W. W. Brown

The Illinois Cook Book

W. W. Brown

The Illinois Cook Book

ISBN/EAN: 9783744781312

Printed in Europe, USA, Canada, Australia, Japan

Cover: Foto ©Lupo / pixelio.de

More available books at **www.hansebooks.com**

THE
ILLINOIS COOK BOOK;

COMPILED BY MRS. W. W. BROWN,

FROM RECIPES

CONTRIBUTED BY THE LADIES OF PARIS,

AND PUBLISHED FOR THE BENEFIT OF

GRACE (EPISCOPAL) CHURCH.

CLAREMONT, N. H.,
PRINTED FOR THE COMPILER BY
THE CLAREMONT MANUFACTURING COMPANY,
1881.

COPYRIGHTED 1881
BY
MRS. W. W. BROWN.

In offering this book to the public we can safely recommend every recipe, as having been *tested, tried and proved*. As they have been furnished by ladies, in Paris (Ills), noted for their practical skill in the culinary department we are not presumptuous in saying that every housekeeper should have the book, and that it is a desirable addition to any library.

TABLE OF WEIGHTS AND MEASURES.

1 qt. of wheat flour = 1 lb.
1 qt. Indian meal = 1 lb. 2 oz.
1 qt. soft butter = 1 lb.
1 qt. broken loaf sugar = 1 lb.
1 qt. powdered white sugar = 1 lb. 1 oz.
1 qt. best brown sugar = 1 lb. 2 oz.
10 eggs = 1 lb.
16 large tablespoons = 1 pt.
8 " teaspoons = 1 gill.
4 " " = $\frac{1}{2}$ gill.
2 gills = $\frac{1}{2}$ pt.
Common size tumbler = $\frac{1}{2}$ pt.
" " teacup = 1 gill.
2 large tablespoons = 1 oz.

ILLINOIS COOK BOOK.

UTENSILS NECESSARY FOR THE KITCHEN.

WOODEN WARE.

Kitchen table, wash bench, wash tubs, (3 sizes) wash board, skirt board, bosom board, bread-board, towel roller, potato masher, wooden spoons, clothes stick, flour barrel covers, flour sieve, chopping bowl, soap bowl, pails, lemon squeezer, clothes wringer, clothes bars, clothes pins, clothes baskets, mop, wood box, and small boards to slice lemons, onions etc. on. Salad knife.

TIN WARE.

Clothes boiler, ham boiler, bread pan, two dish pans, one preserving pan, four milk pans, one quart basin, two pint basins, one covered tin pail, sauce pans with covers, two sizes, two tin cups with handles, one jelly mould, one half pint, one pint mould, one skimmer, one dipper, two funnels—one for jugs and one for cruets, one quart measure, one pint measure, one gill measure, one half pint measure, and they must be broad and low, as such are more easily kept clean; three scoops, bread pans, two round jelly-cake pans, two pie pans, different sizes, one coffee pot, one tea-steeper, one colander, one horse-radish grater, one nutmeg grater, one sieve for straining jelly, egg-beater, cake turner, cake cutter, apple corer, potato cutter, one dozen muffin rings, one soap shaker, ice filter, flour dredge, tea canister, coffee canister, cake, bread, cracker and cheese boxes, crumb tray, and dust pans.

IRON WARE.

Range, one pot with steamer, iron rack to heat plates, soup kettle, porcelain kettle, Tea kettle, large and small frying pans, dripping pans, gem pans, iron spoons of different sizes, one gridiron, one griddle, waffle iron, toasting rack, meat fork, can opener, coffee mill, jagging iron, flat irons, nail hammer, tack hammer, screw driver, ice pick, and iron dish rag.

STONE WARE.

Crocks of various sizes, bowls holding six quarts, four quarts, two quarts, and one pint, six earthen baking dishes, different sizes, pipkins to stew milk or fruit, grease jars.

BRUSHES.

Table brush, two dust brushes, two scrub brushes, one blacking brush for stove, shoe brush, crumb brush, hearth brush, window brush, brooms.

SOUPS.

THE basis of all good soups is the broth of meat. This may be made by boiling the cracked joints of beef, veal or mutton, and is best when cooked the day before it is to be eaten. After putting the meat into the pot, cover it (*only*), with *cold* water, and let it boil, when it should be well skimmed. Before sending to the table, the soup should be strained; after which add the vegetables or seasoning, *cooking all well* together. A good stock for soups may be made from bits of uncooked meat and bones, poultry and the remains of game.

NOODLE SOUP.—Get a good soup bone, put it on the fire with enough cold water to cover it *well*. Season with salt, ginger and nutmeg, one whole onion, and tomatoes if desired. Let it come to a boil, and skim well. Let it boil slowly from three to four hours. Then strain through a fine sieve, put it on to boil; keep filling the pot with *hot* water as it boils away, until an hour before taking off. When it boils put in the noodles; let it boil five minutes and it is done. Fine chopped parsley is considered an addition.

How to make Noodles.—Take one egg, a little salt, flour enough to make a dough that will roll nicely and not *stick;* roll as thin as a wafer. When nearly *dry*, roll an inch and a half wide, cut into noodles as fine as possible. They are ready for use, and will keep for several weeks.

MRS. S. H——.

BARLEY SOUP.—Boil, as with noodle soup; after it is skimmed well, put in nearly a cup of barley which has been previously picked, and washed in cold water—stir often to prevent scorching, season with parsley or leeks. MRS. S. H——.

OATMEAL SOUP.—Boil as before directed, skim well; put in a cup of oatmeal to boil one and a half hours, when it is done; stir often; season with parsley. MRS. S. H——.

FARINA SOUP.—Boil as directed, skim, and strain fifteen minutes before using. Put on to boil and stir in, *very* carefully, half a cup of farina. Let it boil fifteen minutes, when it is done.

MRS. S. H——.

TOMATO SOUP.—Boil as directed, skim. Put on the stove a quart of tomatoes cut up, a little salt; when they are quite done, put through a sieve so fine as to prevent the seeds from going through; strain into the tomatoes as much of the soup as is needed for one meal, put on the stove to boil. Then stir up two eggs with salt and nutmeg, a little parsley and flour to make a thick batter; when the soup boils, drop in dumplings of this batter. When the dumplings swim on top it is done.

MRS. S. H——.

TOMATO SOUP, No. 2.—To one pint of canned tomatoes add one quart of boiling water. Let it boil, then add one teaspoonful of soda. Stir well, and add one pint of sweet milk, with salt, pepper, and *plenty* of butter. Boil, and add a few crackers. MRS. H. M——.

OYSTER SOUP.—For a quart of oysters, after they are strained, pour on a pint of water, and stir with a fork, taking out one at a time, so that they will be entirely free from shell; strain the liquor, put it in a stewpan over the fire, with two or three pieces of mace or nutmeg, a little salt, and a small piece of red pepper. When this boils, put in the oysters, add one teaspoonful of flour rubbed to a paste with two ounces of butter. Add one half pint of cream, boil up once and serve hot.
MRS. H. M——.

GREEN PEA SOUP.—Boil as directed, and skim. Put on a quart of washed, shelled peas, with a little water. Season with salt, pepper, butter and a handful of chopped parsley; let them simmer slowly. Pour in as much of the soup as will be required for one meal; cook one and a half hours, cut some stale light bread in little squares, put in the oven to toast, a nice brown; place in the soup tureen and pour the soup over them.
MRS. S. H——.

FRENCH SOUP.—After boiling as directed, skim. Slice two tomatoes, one onion, two potatoes, one carrot, one turnip, a small handful of cabbage;

add one ear of corn cut off, parsley, celery and leek, if desired, pepper and salt. Put all these vegetables on to cook an hour; stir often; strain, a little at a time, into this, enough soup for one meal, and it is done.

MRS. S. H.———.

CHICKEN SOUP.—Cut up the chicken, and cover well with water, season with salt, pepper and nutmeg; let it boil until the chicken is tender, strain, and put on again to boil without the chicken. For four or five persons, make dumplings of two eggs, chopped parsley, salt and nutmeg. To each egg two heaping spoonfuls of rolled crackers; stir smooth. When the soup boils drop in a teaspoonful at a time of this batter. When the dumplings swim on top they are done. Flour can be used if the rolled cracker is not convenient.

For other dumplings.—Marrow of soup bone, with one egg; season with salt, pepper and nutmeg. Mix well with rolled cracker. Take pieces of this dough the size of a marble, and drop them into the soup. MRS. S. H———.

CORN SOUP.—One small beef bone, two quarts of water, four tomatoes, eight ears of corn; let the meat boil a short time in the water; cut the corn from the cob, and put in the cobs with the cut corn and tomatoes; let it boil half an hour, remove the cobs; just before serving add milk, which allow to boil for a few minutes only; season with salt and pepper.

TOMATO SOUP.—Boil one quart of sweet milk, one quart of hot water, one quart stewed tomatoes with the seeds strained out. Put the tomatoes and water together. Wet one and a half tablespoons of corn starch with a little cold milk, and put into the boiling milk; stir until it thickens; put the milk in the tureen, with a little butter, pepper and salt; pour the tomatoes in last, and serve quickly.

FISH.

AFTER washing them well they should be allowed to remain in sufficient salt water to cover them. Before cooking wipe them dry, dredge them with flour or meal, and season with salt and pepper. Small fish are usually fried; all large fish should be boiled or baked.

To Boil Fish.—Put a small onion inside the fish and tie with a cord. Cover with cold water, and a little vinegar; add a little salt. Let it heat to the boiling point—from two to three minutes will be sufficient time. *Boiling* salt water is best for salmon as it sets the color.

Baked Trout or Blue-Fish.—Make a dressing of two cups of bread crumbs wet with a little milk, an egg, a little fat pork chopped fine (or butter), salt, pepper and nutmeg; mix well together; stuff the body of the fish with this and sew it up. Fry a little pork a nice brown, put it in the pan the fish is to be baked in; add a half teacup of hot water, lay the fish in, cover it with small bits of butter, salt, fine bread crumbs, and bake one or two hours; baste often. Dish the fish, add a little more water, flour and butter; give it one boil and pour it over the fish. Garnish with slices of lemon.

BROILED WHITE FISH, FRESH.—Wash and drain the fish; sprinkle with pepper and lay with the inside down, on the gridiron, and broil over bright, fresh coals. When a nice brown, turn on the other side for a moment, then take up and spread with butter. A little smoke under the fish adds to its flavor; this may be made by putting two or three cobs under the gridiron.

FRIED FISH.—After cleaning the fish, soak it in salt water for a little while, wipe dry with a towel, season with pepper and a little salt. Roll the pieces in meal, and fry in *plenty* of hot lard. When they are nice brown on one side, turn them over, and, when done, pour off all the grease. Let them stand a minute, then serve.   MRS. F. M. P.——.

SMOKED HALIBUT.—Shred in pieces (not too fine) two handfuls of halibut, and put it on the stove in a spider; cover with cold water; let this come to a scald, (be sure not to boil); then turn off the water, and cover again with cold water—scald again; pour off the water. Then take equal quantities of milk and water, enough to cover, thicken with flour, add two well beaten eggs and butter the size of an egg.

FISH BALLS.—One quart of fish that has been freshened and boned, two quarts of cold, boiled potatoes, three slices of salt, fat pork (tried out), chop all finely together. Then add three well beaten eggs, one cup sweet milk, make into balls, and fry brown in the fat that was tried out. Delicious.

MINCED SALT FISH.—Boil the fish and pick all the skin and bones out the day it is boiled, as it is most easily done when it is warm. Next day chop it fine, also any cold potatoes left of a previous dinner. Lay three or four slices of salt pork in a spider, and let them fry a crisp brown, take them out, put in the fish and potatoes, and one gill of milk; stir carefully so as not to disturb the sides and bottom, else a brown crust will not form. Stir in a small piece of butter, when nearly done; loosen the crust from the sides, and turn on a hot dish. It should come out whole, and nicely browned.

OYSTERS.

MEDIUM sized, plump oysters are preferable to very large ones, and the simplest way of cooking them is the best. It should be remembered that over-cooking spoils the flavor of oysters, and makes them indigestible. First, they will grow plump, then the edges will ruffle, *and any further application of heat will shrink and toughen* them into tastelessness.

OYSTERS ON THE SHELL.—Wash the shells and put them on hot coals, or upon the top of a hot stove, or bake them in a hot oven; open the shells with an oyster knife, taking care to lose none of the liquor, and serve quickly on hot plates, with toast. Oysters may be steamed in the shells and are excellent, served in the same manner.

OYSTER SOUP.—Put a quart of oysters to heat in their own liquor; when the edges begin to ruffle, skim them without delay into a hot dish, and add to them, a tablespoonful of butter cut into small bits. To the liquor in the saucepan, put three or four cups of milk or cream, and season to taste with salt and pepper. A few finely broken crackers must be added, just before serving.

For Oyster Soup No. 2 see page 9. Try it—Delicious.

CREAM OYSTERS ON THE HALF SHELL.—Pour into the saucepan a cup of hot water, another of milk, and one of thick cream, with a little salt; set the saucepan into a kettle of hot water until it just boils, then stir in two table spoonfuls of butter, and two table spoonfuls of corn starch stirred into a little cold milk. Have your oyster shells washed and buttered, and a fine large oyster laid in each one; range them closely in a large baking pan, propping them with pebbles or bits of shell, and fill up each shell with the prepared cream, having stirred and beaten it well, first. Bake five or six minutes in a hot oven until a nice brown, and serve in the shell.

BROILED OYSTERS.— Choose large, fat oysters; wipe them very dry, sprinkle them with salt and pepper, and broil upon one of the gridirons with close bars, sold for that purpose. You can dredge the oysters with flour if you wish to have them brown, and many persons fancy the juices are better preserved in that way. Butter the gridiron well, and let your fire be hot and clear; Broil quickly and dish hot, putting a piece of butter upon each oyster as it is taken from the gridiron.

PANNED OYSTERS.—Drain the oysters in a colander, then put them into a very hot frying pan, turn them over in a moment, so as to cook both sides. As soon as they puff up, which will be almost immediately, turn them into a hot platter, which should be standing over a kettle of boiling water with some melted butter, salt and pepper ready in it. Serve immediately. Canned oysters prepared in this way have the flavor of those roasted in the shell.

STEWED OYSTERS.—Put a quart of oysters to heat in their own liquor. When the edges begin to ruffle skim them without delay into a hot dish, and add to them a table spoonful of butter cut into small bits. To the liquor in the saucepan put a teacup of hot cream or rich milk, and season to taste, with salt and cayenne pepper; let it come to a boil, skim and pour it over the oysters. Serve immediately.

ESCALLOPED OYSTERS.—Butter a baking dish and sprinkle a layer of cracker crumbs over the bottom; warm the oysters, very slightly, in their own liquor, then arrange a single layer of them over the crumbs, placing them close together. The juice which clings to each oyster will be sufficient to moisten the cracker, unless you use the latter too liberally. Season with pepper, salt and a *generous* allowance of butter cut into small bits; put on another layer of cracker crumbs, then more oysters and seasoning, and continue alternate layers until the dish is full. Make the top layer of cracker crumbs thicker than the intermediate ones. Cover, and bake in a quick oven, fifteen minutes, then remove the cover and brown the top. A large dish will require longer cooking. A slow oven and too long cooking will completely ruin them.

ESCALLOPED OYSTERS, No. 2.—Crush and roll several handfuls of Boston or other nice crackers; put a layer of them in the bottom of a nicely buttered pudding dish; wet this with a mixture of milk and oyster liquor slightly warmed; next put a layer of oysters; sprinkle with salt, pepper and bits of butter, then another layer of moistened crumbs, and repeat until the dish is full. Let the top layer be thicker than the rest, and beat an egg into a little milk, and pour it over them. Put bits of butter thickly over it, and bake half an hour.

FRIED OYSTERS.—After cleaning them from all particles of shell, sprinkle with salt and pepper. Roll each oyster in finely rolled cracker, then in beaten egg, and in cracker crumbs again; then put into a skillet with plenty of *hot* lard. When done on one side turn over. They are best if prepared a little while before serving.

OYSTER TOAST.—Put a small tablespoonful of butter into a frying pan, and when it melts add a quart of oysters with their juice and a teaspoonful of corn starch rubbed smooth with half table spoonful of butter. Beat an egg and mix it gradually with half a cup of hot milk. Stir the oysters with the corn starch until the juice is smooth and thick, then remove the frying pan from the fire, and add the beaten egg and milk; season with salt and pepper. Return to the fire long enough for the egg to set, but *do not let it boil* or the milk will curdle.

Arrange some slices of buttered toast on a hot platter, over which place the oysters, and serve immediately.

OYSTER TOAST, No. 2. Steam two quarts of oysters until they ruffle. Boil a half cupful of cream thickened with a teaspoon of corn starch previously wet with cold milk. Heat one half cup oyster liquor; season this with salt and pepper; make several pieces of toast, lay them on a flat dish and put on the oysters: then pour over the cream and liquor mixed together at the last moment.

MRS. C. W. L——.

OYSTER OMELETTE. — Whisk six eggs to a stiff froth; add, by degrees, one gill of cream. Beat them well together; season with salt and pepper. Have ready one dozen fine oysters, cut in halves, pour the eggs in a pan of hot butter, drop the oysters over it as equally as possible; fry a slight brown, and serve hot.

OYSTER SALAD.—Drain a quart of oysters from their liquor and cut each one into four pieces; cut one or two heads of blanched celery into small pieces. Do not chop either celery or oysters but use a sharp knife. When prepared set them in separate dishes in a cool place, and, just before serving, mix them carefully together and place them in the dish in which they are to remain.

OYSTER MACARONI.—Boil macaroni in a cloth to keep it straight. Put a layer, seasoned with butter, pepper and salt, in a dish, then a layer of oysters:

alternate until the dish is full. Mix some grated bread with a beaten egg, spread it over the top, and bake. Grated cheese over the macaroni is considered an improvement.

BEANS AND OYSTERS.—Boil beans until ready for the baking: season plentifully with pepper, salt, butter and bits of pork if liked: put a layer of beans into quite a deep baking dish then a layer of raw oysters, and so on until the dish is nearly full, pour over it a teacupful of the oyster liquor and bake one hour.

BREAKFAST AND SUPPER.

CREAM OR MILK TOAST.—Boil a quart of new milk or cream, and thicken with a tablespoonful of flour mixed with three spoonfuls of cold milk, add a little salt and, if milk is used, a little butter; stir steadily until well mixed. Toast slices of bread quickly, of an even brown on both sides. Dip them into the milk, and let them remain a minute. Then lay them in a hot dish, with a cover, and pour over them the remainder of the milk.

PLAIN TOAST.—Toast slices of light bread, an even brown on both sides, and dip each slice, *for a second only*, into a pan of *boiling* water with a little salt in it. As you place each slice into a covered dish, spread bountifully with butter.

MRS. W. W. B———.

MUSH.—Put into a milk boiler about two quarts of water; let it boil, stir into it a large coffee cup of Indian meal wet with some cold water, and let it boil about five minutes; stir well, and add meal if necessary, until very stiff. Let it boil half an hour. Butter a dish and turn the hot mush into it. Next morning turn out on the bread board, (it should be nearly as hard as bread,) cut into slices a half inch thick. Have the griddle hot and well buttered. Fry a nice brown.

GRAHAM MUSH.—Take one quart of boiling hot water, one teacup of corn meal, one teacup of graham flour, one half teaspoon of salt, boil well and put in a dish to cool.

MUSH BREAD.—Put a pint of sweet milk in a sauce pan, and, when it comes to a boil, make a thin mush with corn meal. Cook it done and set it aside to cool, beat in one egg at a time, until you put in three, add piece of butter size of an egg, a little salt. Put in a deep dish and bake. It must be eaten as soon as baked.

OATMEAL.—Place plenty of water on the stove in a milk boiler, and put in the required amount of oatmeal, with a little salt. It should be stirred frequently and cooked one or two hours. Many persons prefer it steamed. To be eaten with sugar and rich cream.

PAWN-HOUSE.—Take a soup bone with plenty of meat on it, put it into a kettle of cold water; remove the scum which rises on top; then boil until the meat falls from the bone; remove the bones after scraping every particle of gristle and marrow from them. Chop up your meat and return it to the kettle, which you must keep three quarters full; salt and pepper to taste, then thicken with corn meal as you do mush; stir until the meat is thoroughly impregnated with the meal, then turn out on a dish to cool, slice and fry brown.

BREAKFAST DISH.—Take slices of dry bread, moisten in milk or water, have ready two well beaten eggs seasoned with salt and pepper, into which dip the bread, and fry it in hot lard.

BITS OF MEAT, HOMINY, MUSH, OR ANYTHING LEFT AFTER A MEAL.—Chop fine, add as many eggs as there are persons to eat, a little salt and flour, and a spoonful or two of sweet cream or milk. Beat well together, and fry in little cakes, in butter or beef drippings.

BREAKFAST CAKES.—If after a boiled chicken you have gravy left, mince the pieces of chicken and mix with it. Pour it over as much old bread as it will soak through, and set it away over night. In the morning, cut it in slices and carefully fry it in butter to a rich brown.

DRY BREAD AND BISCUITS.—Take the pieces and put them in a pan in a cool oven. When perfectly dry and crisp, roll fine, and put away for use; nice for scallopping oysters, potatoes, tomatoes or dredging veal after it has been rolled in beaten egg.

DRY BREAD CAKES.—Soak in warm water until perfectly soft, mash fine with a spoon, add four or five eggs, pepper and salt, beat all thoroughly together. It must be stiff enough to drop from the spoon and form a round cake; if too stiff, add a little water. Fry in *plenty* of hot lard or butter.

BREAKFAST STEW.—Cut the scraps of meat left into small bits; lay them in the skillet with a small bit of butter; dredge with flour; let the meat brown, adding a little water now and then to prevent burning. When well browned, add three sliced potatoes, cold or raw, one sliced onion, and one pint of hot water; stew until the vegetables are done; there should be nearly a pint of gravy when done—if necessary, add water.

SCOTCH STEW.—Four pounds of lean beef passed through a sausage mill, one onion chopped fine, half a teaspoon of salt, pepper to taste. Place in a covered vessel with one teacup of boiling water. Let it stew slowly three or four hours; just before taking off, add butter, size of an egg. Add water when necessary.

HASH.—Put one and a half teacups of boiling water into a sauce pan, mix a tablespoonful of flour with a little cold water, pour it into the pan, and let it cook three minutes; add salt, pepper and butter, chop the cold meat into hash, put it into a tin pan, pour the gravy over it, and let it thoroughly heat, but not cook. If preferred, add equal quantities of cold, boiled, chopped potatoes, and, if you have any, the gravy left of yesterday's meat, and you will need less butter.

HASH—No. 2.—Chop fine some cold beef, or pieces of steak that is juicy, and put in the skillet on the fire, with plenty of water; slice three or four large potatoes, raw, and put into the skillet; also chop as much onion as you like, season with salt and pepper, a good sized lump of butter and a half gill of cream. Let it boil until the potatoes are thoroughly done. If you like the gravy thickened. sprinkle a little flour in the skillet. Very good.

MRS. B———.

Green Tomatoes, Fried.—Slice rather thin, and roll in corn meal; salt and pepper, and place in a hot frying pan, *well buttered; cover closely*, and fry until perfectly tender and nicely browned. If you don't like them at first, try again, as they sometimes require a cultivated taste.

Corn Fritters.—To eight large full ears of corn, *grated*, or shaved thin and scraped, add a little salt and pepper, a tablespoonful of cream or milk, and four eggs. Beat the yolks with the corn, the whites stiff, and stir all together. Have plenty of hot lard in the skillet; fry in small cakes, dropped from the spoon; after browning on one side turn them. Serve in a platter.

Fried Cucumbers.—Pare, cut into lengthwise pieces, a quarter of an inch thick, and lay in cold or ice water, half an hour. Take out, wipe dry, season with salt and pepper; dredge with flour, and fry a light brown.

Ripe Cucumber Salad. — Wash and pare one dozen ripe, yellow cucumbers, cut them into strips, and take out the seeds; chop them into bits as small as a pea; chop with them, (or separately) twelve large white onions, and six large green peppers *without* the seeds. Mix all well together, and add one teaspoonful of white or black mustard seed, two tablespoonfuls of celery seed. To this mixture pour one teacup of salt. Put the whole into a cotton bag to drain over night. Next morning turn it out, put into jars, and fill up with the coldest strong cider vinegar. Keep it tightly corked from the air, and in four weeks it will be a delicate relish for breakfast or supper. It looks very inviting, as it is white and crisp.

PARSNIP FRITTERS.—Scrape and halve the parsnips; boil tender in hot salted water, mash smooth, picking out the woody bits; add a beaten egg to every four parsnips: salt and pepper to taste, and flour enough to make a thick batter; drop by the spoonful into hot lard and fry brown. Drain into a hot colander, and dish.

POTATO PANCAKES.—Grate six good sized raw potatoes, season with salt and pepper, three eggs not beaten, a tablespoon of flour, a very little milk and a pinch of baking powder. Mix all well together, and fry in a skillet, like pancakes, with plenty of grease. MRS. S. H———.

FRICADELLES.—Take the meat from the soup bones, chop fine, with some onion and parsley; fry a little bread as for dressing, and mix with the pepper and salt, and two eggs. Make into little balls, and fry brown.

FRICADELLES—No. 2. Mix one pound of chopped veal or other meat, two eggs, a little butter, one cup or less, of bread crumbs, one chopped onion; the whole well moistened with warm water, or water from stewed meat, season with salt and pepper. Make into balls and fry brown.
MRS. S. H———.

CROQUETS.—One quart finely chopped beef, one common sized onion, six square crackers, salt and pepper to taste, one teacup of boiling water; make into cakes; beat one egg, and dip cakes in egg and flour, fry in hot lard—excellent.

MRS. K. R———.

MEAT SCALLOPS.—Take small tin patty pans, and line them with mashed potatoes; mince any kind of cold meat, and mix with it a little bread crumbs, minced boiled onion, salt and pepper; moisten with a little cold gravy. Put a layer of this over the potatoes; then a layer of potatoes on top. Smooth nicely and lay small bits of butter on top; brown in a hot oven.

MINCED MEAT ON TOAST.—Chop fine all the cold meat left from dinner, place in a spider with a little hot water; add a little flour and butter, salt and pepper to taste. Heat thoroughly, but not too long. Pour this over slices of toasted bread.

SCALLOPED EGGS.—Mince any kind of cold meat; season with salt and pepper, and a few bread crumbs, cover the bottom of saucers with it, putting in each small bits of butter. Break a fresh egg on top. Set in a hot oven, and when the egg begins to cook, sprinkle a little salt, pepper, and *rolled cracker*. Send to the table hot. Nice for breakfast or lunch.

DELMONICO SAUCE.—Take an ounce of ham or bacon, cut it up in small pieces and fry in hot fat; add an onion and a carrot cut fine, thicken with flour; then add a quart of broth seasoned with salt and pepper, and let it simmer for an hour; skim carefully, and strain; a wineglass of any wine added will be a great improvement. Cold roast boiled beef, or mutton may be cut into small squares, fried brown in butter, and then gently stewed in this sauce.

French Croquettes. -- Veal, mutton, lamb, sweatbreads, and any lighter meats, except chicken and turkey, can be judiciously turned into croquettes. Chop the meat, very fine; chop up an onion and fry it in an ounce of butter; add a tablespoonful of flour, stir well and add the chopped meat, a little broth, salt, pepper and a little nutmeg. Stir two or three minutes, then add the yolks of two eggs, and turn into a dish to cool. When cool, mix well together again. Divide up into parts for the croquettes; roll in bread crumbs. Dip in beaten eggs, then in bread crumbs, and fry crisp, a bright golden color.

Bread Omelette.—One large teacup of bread, one teacup of cream, one teaspoon of butter, four eggs, salt and pepper; fry like an omelette.

Omelette.—Beat five eggs, whites and yolks separately; one tablespoonful of flour, mix smoothly with a cup of milk and a little salt, pour into a buttered spider; when partly done, turn half over.

Tomato Omelette.—One teacup cold tomatoes, stewed; beat up two or three eggs with a tablespoonful of flour. Pour into a well buttered spider and, when well set, fold over and serve at once; to be eaten with butter.

ASPARAGUS OMELETTE.—Steam some fresh cut tender asparagus, and chop fine; mix with the yolks of five eggs and the whites of three, well beaten, and two tablespoonfuls of rich cream. Fry, and serve quite hot.

CHEESE OMELETTE.—Beat six eggs very light, add two tablespoonfuls of cream, butter the size of a walnut, a little chopped parsley, pepper and salt, and two ounces of grated cheese; beat well; butter a pan; cook a light brown, fold over and serve. Shake the pan while cooking.

GRATED HAM SANDWICHES.—Grate finely as much well-cooked ham as you are likely to need, flavor with a little cayenne pepper and nutmeg. Roll out some good puff paste very thin, cut it into two perfectly even portions; prick in one or two places to keep from rising too high, and bake in a quick oven until a golden brown. Then take it out and let it stand till cool; then spread a little fresh butter lightly, over the whole. Now, spread the ham evenly over the paste, and lay the second piece evenly over it. With a sharp knife, cut into small sized sandwiches.

POTATO BALLS.—Mash eight nicely boiled potatoes; add salt, pepper, butter and two tablespoonfuls of cream. Stir well, and make into balls; roll in beaten egg, then in crumbs, and fry in hot lard.

Ham Omelette.—Cut the ham into small dice, put into a frying pan with a little butter; stir well. When nearly cooked, pour in the eggs, which have been previously well beaten; when well set, turn half over and serve. If the ham has been boiled, it should be put in at the same time with the eggs.

Cheese Relish.—One fourth of a pound of fresh cheese cut in thin slices; put in a frying pan and pour over it a large cupful of sweet milk; add a quarter of a teaspoon of dry mustard, pinch of salt, pepper and a little butter; stir the mixture all the time. Roll three crackers very fine, and sprinkle in gradually; then turn at once into a warm dish. Serve immediately.

Eggs—Fried.—Grease a skillet, and, when hot, break in the eggs without disturbing the yolks; sprinkle with salt and pepper, *cover*, and when done to suit, cut with a spoon and serve.

Eggs—Baked.—Butter a pie-pan, and break into it seven or eight eggs, so as not to disturb the yolks; salt and pepper to taste, with a small bit of butter on the top of each egg; place in the oven and let remain until the whites are well set, when they will be done.

Eggs—Scrambled.—For a family of six, beat well ten eggs; have a spider quite hot; put in a piece of butter the size of an egg; when melted, turn in the eggs, stirring all the time, until all are cooked, but not too much done; salt and pepper.

EGGS—SCRAMBLED, NO. 2.—Heat a plate until it is *very, very hot*, place on the table and break into it as many eggs as required; season with salt and pepper; stir until all are cooked. This is a very nice dish for those who do not like eggs too much cooked.

SCALLOPED EGGS.—See page 27.

EGGS FOR LUNCH.—Boil half a dozen or a dozen eggs, (for several hours, which renders them as digestible as soft boiled eggs) until *very* hard; remove the shells and cut in halves length-wise; then chop together some cold, boiled ham, cucumber pickle and the yolks very fine; season with salt, pepper, and sufficient mixed mustard to moisten enough to roll into balls, and lay one in each half of the whites. Place in a dish and garnish with parsley.   MISS A. C——.

A SIMPLE OMELETTE.—Break all your eggs in one plate; *stir* rather than beat up the whites and yolks. To each three eggs put in a teaspoonful of cold water; salt and pepper to taste. Chop *fine* some parsley, put two ounces of butter into a pan, and, when hot, pour in the eggs; just as soon as it is cooked on one side, turn quickly and cook on the other side. Double it over, when you serve it on a *very* hot plate. The cold water in the egg makes the omelet light and moist.

DRINKS.

CHOCOLATE.—For those who use a great deal of chocolate the following is an economical method. Cut a cake into small bits, and put them into a pint of boiling water; in a few minutes set off of the fire, and stir until the chocolate is dissolved; then boil it again gently and pour it into a bowl; set in a cool place; it will keep good eight or ten days. For use, boil a spoonful or two in a pint of milk with sugar.

CHOCOLATE—No. 2.—Put a quarter of a pound of chocolote into two quarts of water; stir frequently until dissolved; give it one boil, add one pint of cream (or one quart of milk) and give it one more boil. Sweeten to taste.

COCOA.—The cracked cocoa is considered the best. Two tablespoonfuls put into a pint of cold water, and boiled two or three hours. Boil it over several times and add a little to it each time; boil the milk by itself.

COFFEE.—First have a good article of coffee; look it over carefully, removing all sticks and stones and black grains; put in a bread pan, and place in a stove oven, having the heat, *at first*, sufficient to expand the grains, and gradually increasing it till the coffee is a dark brown, stirring frequently. *By no means allow it to burn;* on removing it from the oven, stir in a piece of butter as large as a hickory nut, for three pints of coffee; this forms a glazing which excludes the air, preventing it from losing its strength; it also improves it. Place it in a tin pan, and keep it tightly covered. Always put the *cream* in the cup before pouring in the hot coffee, and *stir* the cream while filling the cup. In preparing coffee allow one table spoonful of ground coffee to each person; put the required amount into the coffee pot, put in a little of the white of an egg, and pour in some cold water, stirring well; then pour in the proportionate amount of boiling water; let it boil about twenty minutes, set back off the stove, and settle with a *very little* cold water. Mocha and government Java coffee mixed, one part Mocha, two parts Java, make the most delicious coffee.

TEA.—Allow a teaspoonful of tea to each person, put it into the tea-pot, and pour in one cupful of boiling water to every teaspoonful of tea; if it is *green* tea let it *steep* for a little while, but *not boil*, but if *black* tea it is better to *boil* it. Do not use water that has boiled long for tea. Spring water is best, and filtered water next best for tea.

ICED TEA.—After the tea, made quite strong, is perfectly cold, add ice to each glass. If you like place a slice of lemon in the bottom of each cup before pouring in the tea, and then sweeten to taste.

Soda Cream.—Two and a half pounds of white sugar, one eighth of a pound of tartaric acid, both dissolved in one quart of hot water; when cold, add the beaten whites of three eggs, stirring well; bottle for use; put two large spoonfuls of this syrup in a glass of ice-water, and flavor with vanilla, lemon, pineapple or any flavoring, then add one fourth of a spoonful of bi-carbonate of soda. *An excellent substitute for good soda water.*

MEATS.

GENERAL RULES.—All salt meat should be put on in cold water, that the salt may be extracted while cooking; fresh meat should be put to cook in boiling water; when the outer fibres contract the inner juices are preserved. For making *soup*, put the meat in cold water to extract the juices for the broth. In boiling meats add *hot* water, when more water is needed, and be careful to keep the water on the meat constantly boiling; remove the scum when it first begins to boil; the more *gently* meat boils the more tender it will become. Roast meats require a brisk fire. Baste often.

ROAST BEEF, RARE.—Take a rib or loin roast of seven or eight pounds, rinse it off, season with salt, pepper, flour, and, if liked, a chopped onion. If not fat, take a strip of bacon, place in a pan with a little water, roast one hour, (if preferred quite done two hours), in a hot oven. The seasoning gets through the meat better if the meat is stuck with a knife in a number of places, and the seasoning rubbed into these holes with the finger. *Gravy*— pour off nearly all the grease left in the pan after the meat has been taken up, and mix some browned flour with a little cold water; pour into the pan; set it on the top of the stove and let it boil a few minutes; if too thick add hot water, stirring well.

MRS. S. H——.

FILLET-DE-BOEUF.—Take the whole tenderloin, cut crosswise, in strips, one-half inch apart; between the strips, lay strips of bacon, as long as your finger. Then *rub well* with salt and pepper. Put a little water into the roasting pan and place it in the oven. Into the pan put half of an onion, some cloves, and a piece of butter. Bake half an hour in a quick oven. Thicken the gravy with flour. When done pour in a little sour cream.

MRS. S. H——.

BEEFSTEAK, HAMBURG.—Have a porter-house or loin steak cut thick. Scrape off with a spoon, and wipe clean with a towel; season with salt, pepper, and flour. Cut deep gashes in each side, instead of pounding. Have a skillet with a little *smoking* hot grease, lay in the steak, cover it with finely chopped onion: fry quickly; when brown on one side, turn it over; when brown take it out, pour a little water in the skillet, let it boil until the onion is soft; pour over the steak on the dish.

MRS. S. H——.

Tomatoes put on the steak while cooking, is an improvement.

BEEFSTEAK, FRIED VIENNA.—Have the steak chopped fine in the butcher's shop. Season with salt and pepper. Have a little grease in a very hot skillet, put in pieces about an inch thick and three or four inches square, fry brown on both sides.

MRS. S. H——.

BEEFSTEAK, BROILED.———-Scrape or wipe off, and cut deeply on each side instead of beating it. Season with salt and pepper. Put on to broil; when brown on both sides put on a hot dish and spread well with good butter.

MRS. S. H——.

BEEFSTEAK, BROILED No. 2.—Grease the bars of the broiler with butter, beat or cut the steak, which must be cut thick, season with salt and pepper. Place on the broiler over hot coals without a blaze. As the juice of the meat accumulates on the top of the meat, take off with the fork and pour this juice into a teacup, put on the broiler again and so on until thoroughly done. Place on a hot platter. To the juice in the cup add a big lump of butter and about enough hot, clear coffee to color it a nice brown. Pour this gravy over the steak.

MRS. W. W. B——.

BEEFSTEAK, BROILED, No. 3.—Have a skillet, without any grease, *very, very* hot. After the steak has been prepared and seasoned lay it in the skillet, put a little butter on top and continue to hack it with a knife; turn quite often. When brown on both sides, it is done. Serve with plenty of butter.

MRS. J. H——.

BEEFSTEAK, A LA MOCK DUCK.—Take a good sized round steak, season and prepare as for frying; place in the center as much dressing (made of bread as for fowls) as it will hold. Fold up the sides and fasten the ends with a piece of strong thread; season the outside, with salt, pepper and flour. Place in the bread pan, with some cold water, put in the oven and bake as a roast. When done slice across the end in slices half an inch thick.

DRY BEEF.—Cut in very thin slices. Place in a pan and cover well with tepid water: let it gradually boil, then pour off the water. Sprinkle the beef with pepper, and butter, which let melt and boil for a minute. You may add beaten eggs, or cream and flour worked well together. It may be served on thin slices of toast which has been dipped in boiling water with a little salt in it.

VEAL STEAK.—Wash, and dry with a towel, *pound well*, with a steak-mallet. Season with salt, pepper and flour. Put a good sized spoonful of grease in a hot skillet and lay in the steak with some chopped onions, and fry *quite done*. Make gravy in the usual way—hot water and flour.

MRS. S. H———.

VEAL CUTLETS.—Take two or more cutlets, pound well with a potato masher, then wash and dry them on a clean towel, season with salt and pepper. Have ready a half pint of bread crumbs or rolled cracker. Whisk two eggs, with one gill of milk, and pour over the cutlets, then take out one at a time, dip in the bread crumbs, *pat well*, with the back of a spoon, in order to make the crumbs adhere well to the meat. Put in boiling-hot lard, and fry slowly until well browned on both sides. Serve hot.

VEAL PATTIES.—Three and a half pounds of veal, six small crackers, one tablespoonful of salt, one teaspoonful of pepper, one nutmeg, one slice of pork chopped with the veal, a piece of butter the size of an egg: roll the cracker fine. Mix with the spices and meat. Make into a loaf like bread, put bits butter and grated bread crumbs on the top. Put it into a pan with a little water. Baste frequently while baking; bake two hours. To be eaten cold.

MRS. C. W. L————.

VEAL OMELET.—Three and a half pounds of veal when chopped, six butter crackers, two eggs, a half tea-cup of butter, one tablespoon of salt, one of pepper; chop the veal fine; roll the cracker fine; beat the eggs with the butter. Mix all together with your hand. Make into a loaf, sprinkle over with rolled crackers, and butter; bake three hours; have a little salt, pepper, water and butter in a pan to baste it with afterwards. A small piece of pickled pork is very nice instead of the half cup of butter.

MRS. GEO. B————.

Beef can be substituted for the veal, and baked *one* hour.

To Corn Beef.—To every four gallons of water allow two pounds of brown sugar, and six pounds of salt; boil twenty minutes, taking off the scum. The next day pour it on the meat packed in a pickling tub, pour off this brine, boil and strain every two months, adding three ounces of brown sugar and half a pound of common salt. It will keep good a year. Sprinkle the meat with salt the next day, wipe dry before turning the pickle over it. Let it entirely cover the meat and add four ounces of saltpetre. Canvas lids are excellent, as they admit the air and exclude the flies. Turn the pieces whenever the vessel is uncovered.

Preserving Beef.—For preserving one hundred pounds of beef take six pounds of salt, two ounces of saltpetre, two tablespoonfuls of soda, two pounds of sugar and four gallons of water. Mix well together; sprinkle the bottom of the barrel with salt, put in the beef with very little salt between the layers, pour over the brine and put on a weight to keep all well covered.

Pickled Tongue.—Take a corned ox-tongue and boil it until tender; take off the skin; put it into a stone basin or jar, and cover it with good cider vinegar; add a few allspice, whole pepper corns and cloves—not more than a dozen of each.

Pickled Tongue, No. 2.—To one tongue, two handfuls of salt, a little garlic, one teaspoonful of saltpetre, mixed with the salt, two slices of lemon; rub all on the tongue. Place the tongue in a jar with the seasoning, whole cloves and peppers. To a quart of water add one gill of strong cider vinegar; a heavy stone on top of the plate will keep the tongue thoroughly covered. It is ready for use in two or three weeks. It must be boiled in the usual manner, and peeled before it is ready for the table.   MRS. S. H———.

STEWED TONGUE.—Cut square fillets of bacon, which dredge with a mixture of chopped parsley, salt, pepper, and a little allspice. Lard the tongue with the fillets. Put into a sauce-pan two ounces of bacon cut in slices, four sprigs of parsley, two of thyme, a little garlic, two cloves, two carrots cut in small pieces, two small onions, salt and pepper. Lay the tongue on the whole, wet with a glass of white wine and a glass of broth. Set on a moderate fire and simmer about five hours, keeping it well covered. Put the tongue on a dish and strain the sauce over it.

POTATO EDGING FOR TONGUE.—Mash potatoes and season with butter, pepper, salt and cream; dish in lumps, with a large spoon, and stick a sprig of parsley into each one.

LAMB'S LIVER.—Cut in slices a half inch thick, beat the yolks of two eggs, and dip the slices first in egg then in crumbs; season with salt and pepper, and fry in hot drippings.

TO STEW TRIPE.—Six pounds of tripe; when well parboiled, cut in pieces, and put into water enough to stew; when quite tender, (which may take several hours) add three pints of sweet milk, four tablespoons of flour, two onions, pepper and salt, and three-fourths of a cup of butter. Let them stew fifteen minutes, and it will be ready for use.

TRIPE-A-LA-CREOLE.—Cut two pounds of tripe into thin strips, three inches long and half an inch wide; wash them for a few minutes in tepid water; slice two onions, chop them fine, and put them into a frying pan with a tablespoonful of good butter: take three tomatoes and remove the skins by putting in hot water: when the onion is perfectly brown put on the tomato in slices, a pinch of parsley, pepper and salt. Let this cook six minutes, then add a glassful of white wine. Let it then simmer. Have the tripe now ready, having heated it thoroughly in a sauce pan with a little water. Mix the tripe and sauce together in the sauce pan and let it cook. Serve as hot as possible.

SWEETBREADS, FRIED. After lying in salt and water, put them in cold water a few minutes, then dry on a cloth thoroughly; fry them with little strips of salt pork, or dip in beaten egg and bread crumbs; fry in hot lard—stir one tablespoonful of flour into a half cup of rich cream; let it boil for a few minutes, pour over and serve hot.

SWEETBREADS, STEWED.—Wash, remove all the bits of skin, soak in salt and water one hour, then parboil; when half cooked remove from the fire, cut in small pieces, stew them in a little water until tender, add a piece of butter, a teaspoon of salt and one of flour, and boil up once. Serve on toast, very hot.

SWEATBREADS, BROILED.—Parboil, after soaking in salt water; rub well with butter, and broil; turn often, and dip in melted butter to prevent them from becoming hard and dry.

ROASTED VENISON. A leg of venison should be roasted one and a half to three hours. The dry skin should be taken off, before roasting, with the fingers, not with a knife. The spit should be turned very often; when half done, it should be basted with flour, butter and red wine, very frequently, until done. A *saddle* of venison is much the best piece of the deer; requires half the time to roast it that it does the leg, for it is a much thinner piece. Dress in the same manner as the leg.

VENISON GRAVY.— For a leg of venison take five pounds of coarse beef, boil five or six hours. To three quarts of this liquor add a half pint of port wine, one nutmeg, two teaspoons of powdered cloves, a half pound of butter, a little sugar, and thicken with browned flour; after boiling the beef and spices together, strain, before adding the other ingredients; add mace, and a half pint of brandy if liked. Salt to taste.

A VENISON STEAK.—Cut steaks, from the leg, one inch thick; broil about five minutes, season with salt, pepper and butter; a cupful of the roast venison gravy poured over it, *very hot*, is nice, *or* one half cup of currant jelly thickened with a little browned flour and butter boiled up and turned over the steak.

VENISON PIE.—Take the neck and breast of the venison, cut into small pieces, season with salt, pepper, and a little ground cloves; put into the pie dish as thick as possible, fill up the dish with some venison gravy or a gravy made of flour, butter, hot water, salt and pepper. Put into the oven for half an hour to stew, then add a nice pie-crust and bake half an hour longer.

SAUSAGE.—Ten pounds of fresh pork, six tablespoonfuls of sage, three tablespoonfuls of salt, two or three tablespoons of black pepper.

TO BOIL A HAM.—Prepare the ham the night before, and let it soak all night in cold water: as soon as the water comes to a boil pour it off, and add cold water again; then add a quart of champagne cider, (if this cannot be obtained hard cider will do,) and a few whole spices; cover closely and let it boil slowly until perfectly tender. *Very* nice.

MRS. G. B———.

FRICASSEE OF CALF'S TONGUE.—Boil the tongue one hour: pare and cut into thick slices: roll them in flour and fry in drippings five minutes; put the tongues into a sauce pan, add sliced onion, thyme and parsley; cover with a cupful of soup, or other gravy. Simmer half an hour, covered tightly; take up the tongues and keep them warm; strain the gravy, thicken, put in four or five thin slices of peeled lemon, boil one minute and pour over the fricassee.

STUFFED OR DRESSED HAM.—Mix one quart of grated light bread with a teaspoon each of mace, nutmeg, cloves, allspice, salt, thyme, sweet basil, fat meat, and parsley chopped fine, and a little butter and brandy to soften the dressing. Boil and skin a nice ham, make incisions about an inch apart as deep as possible, and stuff with the above mixture. Spread the yolk of an egg over the top and then grate bread-crumbs thickly over it. Bake until brown. *Very* nice.

CURING HAMS.—Rub salt all over them as soon as cut and laid on a table: the next day brush off and pack in a cask. Put on a pickle made as follows; one quart of salt to one gallon of water: to six gallons of water, one half gallon of molasses and three ounces of saltpetre. Let the hams remain in six or eight weeks, according to size. Smoke to suit, and pack away in salt in a cask. Put in a cool, dry place, and they will keep good all summer.

A LUNCH FOR TRAVELLING.—Chop sardines, ham and a few pickles quite fine; mix with mustard, pepper, catsup, salt and vinegar. Spread between slices of bread nicely buttered.

GRATED HAM SANDWICHES.—See page, 29.

HAM OMELET.—See page, 30.

FOWLS.

ROAST TURKEY.—Clean, and wash out the crop and body of the turkey with soda and water, rinsing it out afterwards; stuff with a force-meat made of bread crumbs, a little cooked sausage, pepper, salt and butter; truss the turkey neatly, lay it in the dripping pan, pour boiling water over it and roast about ten minutes to the pound, after the cooking actually commences. Cook slowly at first, basting often and freely. Ten minutes before taking it up, dredge with flour, and baste with butter; pour off the fat from the top of the gravy; thicken with browned flour, and season; boil once, and serve in a gravy boat. To make *oyster* dressing, take a pint of oysters to five cents worth of crackers rolled fine; wash the oysters and take them out with a fork; strain the liquor into the crackers, put in the oysters; season with salt, pepper and butter.

Fowls should *always* be killed the *day before* they are used. Mix the seasoning—salt, pepper and ginger—in a saucer, and rub the fowl *well*, inside and outside, with it, the night before it is to be used. If the fowl is not fat enough use strips of bacon or butter. Put in a roasting pan with a quart of water, baste frequently while cooking; when done thicken the water with flour, for gravy. Ducks, chickens and geese are all baked alike.

Dressing for Fowls.—Soak some stale bread in *cold* water; squeeze out well; have some butter hot in a skillet, cut into it finely chopped onion, put in the bread, let it fry about fifteen minutes, stirring all the time. Take it out into a bowl. When cooled season with pepper, salt, nutmeg and chopped parsley; if preferred chop the liver and heart fine, break two or four eggs, mix all with the bread with the back of a spoon so it will work nicely together. Place it in the fowl.

MRS. S. H——.

To Roast a Goose.—Take a young goose, pick and singe and clean it well; boil half an hour, to take out the strong, oily taste, then make the dressing with two ounces finely chopped onion, one ounce green sage, chopped fine, one large coffee cup bread crumbs, some mashed potatoes, pepper, salt, butter the size of a walnut, yolk of one or two eggs; mix these well together, and stuff the goose; do not fill entirely, as the stuffing requires room to swell. It will take one and a half hours to roast it thoroughly. *Sauce*—Put into a saucepan one tablespoonful of made mustard, half a teaspoonful of red pepper, one glass port wine and a gill of the gravy; mix and warm, and pour over the goose just before serving.

MRS. S. H——.

CHICKEN, A-LA-MODE.—Put the chicken on in just enough cold water to cover it, and boil until the bones easily leave the flesh; separate the meat from the bones and boil the gravy to a jelly; chop the meat fine, mix it with pepper, salt and spice; boil some eggs hard; slice thin; line a deep dish with them; put in the chicken and gravy; when cold turn on to a dish, to be sliced thin. Nice for tea or for lunch.   MRS. C. W. L——.

FRICASSEE—YOUNG CHICKENS—After the chickens are cleaned, cut off the wings and flatten with the rolling pin; do the same with the back and breast (cutting each in two pieces, the back crosswise;) clean the giblets nicely, and, having washed all together, in cold water slightly salted, put them in a stew pan with just enough water to cover them, or half milk and half water; add a few pepper-corns, a little mace and a little salt; (a head of young lettuce is an improvement). Cover the stew pan and let the chicken boil until quite tender; strain off half a pint of the liquor into another saucepan; add half a pint of boiling milk, set it on the fire, stir into it a tablespoonful of butter rolled in flour, and continue to stir, until quite smooth; add a little nutmeg; after it is taken off stir in any kind of flavoring—vinegar or wine. Arrange the chickens in a deep dish, pour the gravy over them and send to the table covered.

FRICASSEE—YOUNG CHICKEN, No. 2—Clean the chicken, and cut it up as if for frying; place the pieces in a skillet filled with water and add a little salt; when the water is all out put in a large tablespoonful of butter and some pepper; the pieces will fry a light brown on one side, when turn over and fry a nice brown on the other side; if necessary add more butter. When done, take up the chicken, and make plenty of gravy with flour and hot water, in the usual manner. This is a good plan for those who are very fond of *fried* chicken, when the chicken is a little too old to fry in the usual way.

Birds are dressed, split open in the back and baked in the oven or *broiled*. While they are broiling, they should be lifted from the broiling iron occasionally and dipped in a gravy of melted butter, pepper and salt, flavored strongly with port wine.

SAUCES, SALADS AND PICKLES.

SAUCE FOR CHICKEN SALAD, SLAW OR LETTUCE.—Two eggs, two tablespoonfuls of sugar, one half teaspoon of ground mustard, one half teaspoon of pepper, one half teaspoon of salt. Beat all well together, add one teacup of vinegar, boil all together in a cup set in hot water, and, when thick as custard, add a lump of butter the size of a hen's egg.

MRS. KATE R————.

COLD SAUCE—One fourth pound of butter beaten to a cream; add gradually one fourth pound sugar; add lemon juice; beat till very white; or one cup sugar, piece butter size of an egg, beat to a cream; add one glass of wine, and the white of one egg beaten to a stiff froth.

PUDDING SAUCE—One gill of milk, or wine and water, one fourth pound sugar, two eggs, beaten to a stiff froth; pour the liquid, boiling hot, into the eggs and sugar. Nutmeg.

LEMON SAUCE—One cup sugar, one half cup butter, one egg, one lemon-juice and grated rind, three tablespoonfuls of boiling water, put into a pan; set over the steam, and stir till it thickens.

SAUCES, SALADS AND PICKLES.

CHILI SAUCE.—One large onion, two red peppers, six large tomatoes, one tablespoon of salt, one teaspoon of ginger, one teaspoon of cinnamon, one teaspoon of cloves, two tablespoons of brown sugar, and two teacups of vinegar. Boil slowly two hours and stir well.

MRS. G. L————.

PUDDING SAUCE. — One pint of boiling water, a half pint of sugar, a half tablespoon of butter, one tablespoon of flour or corn starch, one tablespoon of vinegar. Berry juice gives a good flavor and a nice color.

MRS. GEO. L————.

SALAD DRESSING.—Four eggs beaten well, two tablespoons mixed mustard, one tablespoon hard butter, five tablespoons vinegar and one teaspoon salt; cook.

MRS. M. P. J————.

RHUBARB SAUCE.—Make a syrup of sugar and water, as rich or as thin as you please, only it *must* be *syrup*. Skim. Cut the rhubarb into inch pieces without peeling, add to the syrup and stew until tender. Beware of adding lemon, ginger, eggs, or butter to qualify the flavor of pieplant.

SALAD DRESSING.—Beat two eggs with a teaspoon of mixed mustard, four teaspoons of melted butter or salad oil; add, by degrees, two teaspoons of salt, two heaping teaspoons of sugar, one half teacup of vinegar, mix well, set on the stove till it thickens. *Be sure not to let it boil.* When cool stir in two teaspoons of rich cream. Set it away to get quite cold; pour this dressing over the salad just before sending to the table.

Foam Sauce.—One teacup of butter, two and a half teacups of sugar, two large tablespoons of flour; beat all to a cream, then pour in one half pint boiling water; boil ten minutes; beat the white of an egg to a stiff froth and stir in just before taking off the stove.

Salad Dressing. Rub the yolks of four hard boiled eggs to a smooth paste, then add two tablespoons of melted butter, one teaspoon of salt, one tablespoon of white sugar, pinch of pepper, one tablespoon of Worcestershire sauce and one cup of vinegar. Mix all carefully and pour over.

Sauce for Cake or Pudding.—One pint of water, sweeten to taste; a lump of butter size of an egg, a dozen cloves, teaspoon of vanilla extract; put on the fire to boil, and, when boiling, stir in a heaping teaspoon of corn starch, which has been previously mixed with cold water.

MRS. W. W. B———.

Chicken Salad.—Take a fine bunch of white celery, four or five heads, scrape and wash clean; reserve the green leaves, shred the white part like straws and lay in a glass dish in the form of a nest. Mince all the white meat, without skin, and put it into the nest. Make a salad dressing thus: rub the yolks of two hard boiled eggs to a smooth paste with a dessert spoon of salad oil or melted butter;

add to it a teaspoon of white sugar and a pinch of salt, and put to it gradually a cup of strong vinegar. Make a wreath of the delicate green leaves of the celery, around the edge of the nest, between it and the chicken — pour the dressing over the chicken when ready to serve: if poured over too soon it will discolor the celery. White heart lettuce can be used for the nest.

CHICKEN SALAD, No. 2.—Take one chicken, stew it, but not too tender; when cold cut it into small pieces size of a pea; take nice crisp celery, put it in water for a while; cut it in little pieces; boil a few eggs hard; put the yolks in a bowl and stir with two tablespoons of dry mustard; cut the whites fine; take a handful of capers, some pepper, salt, vinegar and salad oil, or melted butter, and a little water. Mix well, garnish with celery and hard boiled eggs. Excellent.
MRS. S. H———.

CHICKEN SALAD, No. 3.—One boiled chicken, one half cup melted butter, five hard boiled eggs, (yolks) one half pint vinegar, one teaspoon dry mustard, one half teaspoon of red pepper, one teaspoon of salt, two heads of celery and a pint of chopped cabbage.
MRS. A. B. R———.

CHICKEN SALAD, No. 4.—Two large chickens, eight heads celery, ten eggs, one teacup of olive oil or melted butter, one tablespoon of mustard, one teaspoon cayenne pepper, one teacup of vinegar, and salt to taste. Mash the yolks thoroughly with the oil, or butter and add salt, pepper and vinegar. Boil the chickens until the bones can be taken out. When cold pick to pieces; chop the celery, (part cabbage is better,) mix well, stir lightly with a silver fork. Pour the mixture over when ready for use—not before.

MRS. GEO. L——.

MAYONNAISE SAUCE.—Put the beaten yolks of eight fresh eggs in a salad bowl and add white pepper, a little grated nutmeg and a teaspoon of salt. Then pour slowly and steadily one and a half pints of best olive oil into the bowl, stirring all the time; as the parts become thick, add, a teaspoonful at a time, enough of good vinegar to reduce to the proper consistency. The salads upon which this sauce may be used can be garnished with slices of hard boiled eggs.

WINE SAUCE.—One fourth pound butter, beaten to a cream with one fourth pound sugar. Boil one gill of wine or brandy and half a gill of water mixed; pour over the sugar and butter. Send to the table immediately.

CELERY SAUCE.—Chop fine one head of celery, put it into a sauce pan with a pint of water, a little salt, and a few peppercorns. Boil it well. Braid a tablespoon of flour with two ounces of butter; stir it in with a half cup of cream or milk, add the seasoning, and boil up well. This is nice with boiled fowl or turkey.

SAUCES, SALADS AND PICKLES. 55

BREAD SAUCE FOR BIRDS.—A very small cup of chopped onions boiled in water till quite soft, and the water strained off. Boil one pint of milk, pour it over a cup of bread crumbs, two ounces of butter, a little salt, pepper and mace; stir in the onion, boil once and serve hot.

DRAWN BUTTER SAUCE.—Two ounces of butter beaten smooth, one tablespoonful of flour, one teacup of boiling water; mix all together, set over the fire and stir constantly until it boils; add salt, pepper and hard boiled egg chopped fine; a half pint of oysters may be added instead of egg, for boiled fowl.

MUSTARD.—One cup of vinegar, two tablespoons of sugar, one tablespoon of butter, half a tablespoon of celery seed. Mix well, let it come to a good boil, then stir in two tablespoons of mustard.

TO MIX MUSTARD.—Pour enough boiling water on the mustard to scald it thoroughly and form a thick paste; add a pinch of salt, and thin to proper consistency with good vinegar. Try it.

MRS. C. W. L——.

VEAL SALAD.—Boil veal till very tender, chop fine and stir into it a nice salad dressing; put it in a shallow dish and garnish with slices of lemon and celery. A little chopped cabbage or lettuce may be added, if desired. Boiled ham, chopped and seasoned, and served in the same manner, is a very nice dish.

Potato Salad.—Select new potatoes, or old ones that are not very mealy; boil them and cut into small pieces; while warm season with plenty of butter, salt, pepper, a little chopped onion and vinegar; set away to get cold for supper. Cold beans, peas, beets etc., left from dinner are *very* nice prepared in this way for supper.

Mayonnaise Sauce, No. 2.—Yolks of two raw eggs (not a particle of the whites, else your sauce will curdle) one and a half mustard spoonfuls of mixed mustard beaten together; add very slowly the best salad oil, stirring constantly, until you can reverse the dish without spilling; then add one tablespoonful of vinegar, cayenne and black pepper to taste, and a half teaspoonful of salt; stir briskly until quite light colored, and serve on lobster, lettuce or fish.

Horseradish Sauce.—Two teaspoonfuls of made mustard, two of white sugar, half a teaspoonful of salt and a gill of vinegar; mix and pour over grated horse radish.

Celery Flavoring—Soak for two weeks half an ounce of celery seed in a pint of brandy. A few drops of this will flavor a pint of soup nearly as well as if a head of celery was stewed in it.

Vanilla Extract. — One gallon proof spirits (not alcohol) to one pound vanilla beans; crush the beans in a mortar, and put in the spirits; let it stand five or six weeks, and strain off as wanted.

LEMON EXTRACT.—One pint of alcohol to two ounces of oil of lemon; let it stand five or six weeks, shaking occasionally.

CHERRY OR CURRANT SAUCE.—Four pounds of cherries or currants, two pounds of sugar, one cup of vinegar, half an ounce of cinnamon, or other spices if preferred; cook slowly about an hour.

MRS. C. W. L———.

GOOSEBERRY CATSUP.—Eight pounds of ripe or partially ripe fruit, four pounds brown sugar, one pint of good vinegar, two ounces *each* of fine cloves and cinnamon tied in a bag. Boil the berries and sugar for three or four hours, then add the spice, boil a little longer, put in a jar and cover well. Will keep two years by occasionally scalding and adding a little vinegar and spice.

TOMATO CATSUP. — Splendid. Take ripe tomatoes, and, having quartered them, let them stand in a stone jar over night; in the morning, throw away the water produced. Rub them through a sieve, and to every pint of tomatoes add a pint of strong vinegar, an ounce of onions sliced fine, one fourth of an ounce of ground black pepper; ginger, cloves, and allspice, half a drachm each; half an ounce of salt. Boil the whole together, until each ingredient is tender, then rub through a sieve with a wooden spoon, and to each pint add the juice of two lemons. Boil until it is of the thickness of cream. Bottled and sealed it will keep for years.

MRS. C. W. L———.

Recipe for *one* gallon of Tomato catsup. Eight pints tomatoes, eight pints vinegar, half pound onions, two ounces ground pepper, one fourth ounce each of allspice, cloves, ginger and cinnamon and four ounces salt.

MRS. C. W. L———.

SLICED TOMATO PICKLE. — Take one gallon of sliced tomatoes that are just turning white, scald them in salt water, until a little tender; take one teaspoon of pepper, same each of mace, cloves, mustard and cinnamon, four teaspoons of white mustard, one pod green pepper, four onions chopped fine, and half a pint grated horse-radish. Mix all together, add one pound of sugar, and cover with vinegar.

RIPE TOMATO PICKLES. — One peck of ripe tomatoes; prick them with a large needle, lay them in strong salt and water eight days. Then take them out of the brine and lay them in vinegar and water, for twenty-four hours. Scald a dozen small onions in vinegar and stand the whole away to get cold. Drain the tomatoes, add them to the cold onions and vinegar with a wine-glassful of mustard-seed and half an ounce of cloves.

CUCUMBER PICKLES.—One gallon of vinegar, a small teacup of salt, six red peppers, a tablespoonful of celery seed, and small pieces of alum and horse-radish. Wash and wipe the cucumbers, fill the jars, put a weight on top, tie up close, and in a few days they will be ready for use.

CUCUMBER PICKLES, NO. 2.—Wash your cucumbers with care, place them in jars and make a weak brine, (a handful of salt to a gallon and a half of water). When scalding hot pour over the cucumbers and cover; repeat this process three mornings in succession, taking care to skim thoroughly. On the fourth day have ready a porcelain kettle of vinegar to which has been added a lump of alum, size of a walnut. When scalding hot put in as many pickles as the vinegar will cover, do not let them boil, but skim off as soon as scalded through, and replace them with others, adding each time a small piece of alum. When through with all the pickles, throw out this vinegar and replace with good cider vinegar; add spices, mustard-seed, and red peppers. Place them in stone jars; and over them pour the hot spiced vinegar; seal and put away the jars not needed for immediate use. Horse-radish root cut lengthwise and placed on top of pickles will impart a pleasant taste and also prevent mold.

TOMATO CATSUP—RIPE.—Boil one peck of ripe tomatoes, fifteen minutes, without removing their skins, and strain through a sieve. Put into a little bag one teaspoonful of cloves, (whole) one tablespoon each of ground cinnamon, allspice and black pepper, and put these with a pint of good vinegar into the strained tomatoes, and boil the whole carefully from three to five hours. When sufficiently boiled add one tablespoon ground mustard, one teaspoon black and same of red pepper.

TOMATO PICKLES.—Thirty-six green tomatoes, ten green peppers, (without the seeds) ten large onions, eight cups vinegar, six tablespoons of sugar, three tablespoons of salt, celery and mustard-seed to taste ; *scald well* together.

CUCUMBER CATSUP.—One dozen large cucumbers, five large onions; grate each separately, and soak in salt water one hour, then squeeze the juice out; with the pulp put red pepper and spices to taste ; add sufficient vinegar to thin properly.

MRS. J. H. M———.

CHILI SAUCE.—One large onion, two red peppers, six large tomatoes, all chopped fine, one tablespoon of mustard, one each of cinnamon, cloves, and salt ; two tablespoons of brown sugar and two teacups of vinegar. Boil slowly two hours. This is very nice for cold meats.

MRS. J. H. M———.

GREEN TOMATO PICKLES.—Slice, salt and let stand over night, two gallons of green tomatoes; then squeeze out, and add twelve onions chopped fine, two quarts vinegar, two heads cabbage chopped fine, one quart sugar, horseradish chopped or scraped, one tablespoonful cloves and one of allspice, two tablespoons of mustard and two of black pepper. Mix all well and boil one hour; can it, and it will keep as long as you wish.

MRS. J. H. M———.

MANGOES. — To stuff one dozen mangoes, take one cup each of white and black mustard seed, one handful of horse radish, one teaspoonful each of cloves, mace, cinnamon, black pepper, celery seed, and one cup of sugar ; mince a small head of cabbage fine, pour hot vinegar over it and let it stand half an hour. Then drain off, and when cold put the mixture together, adding small beans and cucumbers, and fill the mangoes. Place them in the kettle with steam up, and scald gently with the vinegar.

Chow-Chow.—Twenty-four large green tomatoes, eight onions and twelve (seedless) peppers; chop these fine, then add four tablespoons of salt, eight tablespoons of sugar, four teaspoons each of cloves, cinnamon, and ginger and eight teacups of vinegar. Boil all together slowly for two hours.

Chili Sauce.—One peck of ripe tomatoes chopped fine; strain the water off; one cup of chopped onions, one cup of sugar, one cup of mustard seed, one cup of grated horseradish, a fourth of a cup of salt, two peppers chopped fine, one teaspoon each of cloves, mace and cinnamon, two tablespoons of celery seed, three pints of vinegar. Mix together and it is done; bottle for use.

Ripe Tomato Pickles—Sour.—One pound of brown sugar to a four gallon jar of tomatoes; peel the tomatoes, puncture with a fork, and put in layers in the jar; sprinkling a little sugar over each layer. Put a light weight on top and keep in a moderately warm place for a few weeks. They make their own vinegar, and are sharp pickles. Brown sugar is best.

English Mixed Pickles.—One half peck of small green tomatoes, three dozens small cucumbers, two heads of cauliflower, a half peck of small, tender beans, (string,) six bunches of celery, six green peppers, and a quart of small white onions; chop the vegetables quite fine, sprinkle with salt and let stand over night. To six or seven quarts of vinegar add one ounce each of ground cloves, allspice and pepper, two ounces of turmeric and a fourth pound of mustard seed. Let the vinegar and spice come to a boil, put in the vegetables and scald until tender and a little yellow.

RIPE TOMATO CATSUP.—Pour boiling water on a peck of very ripe red tomatoes, to slip the skins off. Remove all bad spots or green lumps from about the stem end. Boil slowly for three hours in a porcelain vessel, stirring often from the bottom. Then add four tablespoons of ground black pepper, three heaping tablespoons of good mustard, six medium sized red peppers chopped, and half a tablespoonful of cloves, and the same of allspice thoroughly stewed in the best cider vinegar. Simmer the whole, half an hour, and strain through a common flour sieve; bottle hot and seal air tight. This makes one gallon of catsup.

GREEN TOMATO SOY.—To one peck of green tomatoes add three large onions and six good green peppers. Slice all together, leaving out the blossom ends of the tomatoes and the seeds of the peppers. Put all together into three pints cider vinegar and two pints water. Let it boil five minutes. Then strain out the tomatoes, etc., and throw the vinegar away; now take two quarts fresh vinegar, add two cups brown sugar, one cup mustard, made smooth with cold water, one tablespoon each of ground cinnamon, cloves and allspice, and three tablespoons of salt. Let this boil up, and pour it over the tomatoes. Put in covered stone jars, and it will be ready for use when cold.

CHOW-CHOW—Warranted to be good. One peck of green tomatoes peeled, one large head of cabbage, half a dozen good sized onions, chop fine and salt separately at night. In the morning drain off the water from the vegetables, and mix them thoroughly, adding six green and two ripe peppers. Take as much vinegar as will cover them. Let it come to a boil. Put the vegetables in the vinegar and let them scald a few minutes, then take them out and put them in a jar, adding a little black pepper, cinnamon, and cloves. Throw away half the vinegar used and add new vinegar and a pint of sugar to it. When boiling hot pour it over the vegetables.

APPLE SAUCE. Fill a quart bowl with alternate layers of sliced apples and sugar; add half a cup of water, and cover with a saucer held down with a weight. Bake slowly three hours, and let it stand till cold. Or: pare and core sweet apples, place them in a porcelain kettle, with a little water and sugar, steam or stew them slowly, by covering tightly; when soft enough to be penetrated by a straw, remove the apples carefully, one by one, to a glass dish; add a cup of white sugar to the syrup in the kettle, boil it a few minutes, then pour it over the apples. Beat two or three whites of eggs to a stiff froth, place the apples in pyramid form, pour the whites over them and, lastly, sprinkle with finely sliced lemon peel.

SWEET PICKLES.

For Jellies.—Take six pounds of dried apples and six gallons of cold water and let them soak twelve hours, then strain through a flannel bag; add to each pint of the juice one pound of grape sugar, and one ounce of Cooper's sheet gelatine; boil twenty-five minutes and flavor to taste.

Apple Butter.—Take four pounds of dried apples, two pounds of dried pumpkin; soak them twelve hours, then add one gallon of gluco or grape sugar; one quart of boiled cider, one quart of golden syrup, six pounds of New Orlean's sugar, one fourth of a pound of Cooper's gelatine, a little spice mixed to suit the taste. Boil gently for one hour, stirring all the time.

Apple Butter, No. 2.—Nine gallons of fresh cider boiled down to six gallons; ten gallons of apples, pared and cored; ten lbs. of sugar, cinnamon to suit the taste. Add sugar and cinnamon just half an hour before taking up. Boil all, three or four hours, stirring all the time.   MRS. GEO. L——.

Spiced Fruit.—Seven pounds of fruit, three pounds of sugar, one pint of vinegar, allspice, cloves and stick cinnamon. Boil the syrup three mornings and pour it over the fruit; the third morning cook the fruit until tender.   MRS. GEO. L——.

SWEET PICKLES.

Any kind of spiced fruit syrup, after the fruit is all used out, is better to put in mince meat than boiled cider, therefore it should be saved for that purpose. MRS. L——.

SPICED PEACHES.—One peck of peaches, two quarts of vinegar, four pounds of sugar, three nutmegs, one tablespoonful each of cloves and cinnamon; after paring the peaches, place in a jar, strewing spices through them. Boil vinegar and sugar together, and pour over them, three days in succession; the fourth day boil all together for twenty minutes.

GREEN TOMATO SWEET PICKLES.—Take a quart of vinegar and six pounds of sugar, with one ounce each of cloves, cinnamon and allspice, and boil them together. Then take medium sized tomatoes, have them whole and green, stick cloves around in them and boil them in the syrup until tender. Put them into a jar and cover them with the syrup.

SPICED PEACHES, No. 2.—One Peck of fruit, five pounds of sugar, one pint of cider-vinegar; tie in a thin muslin bag one ounce each of cinnamon, cloves and whole spice; make a syrup of the sugar and vinegar, add the fruit and spice; boil half an hour, and seal while hot.

MUSKMELON PRESERVES.—Take a ripe muskmelon, remove the seeds, peel and cut in pieces; put into a stone jar and cover with scalding vinegar; let them stand until next day, when pour off the vinegar, heat it and pour it on them again; do the same every day until the fourth day. Weigh the melon and to every five pounds add three pounds of sugar, one quart of the vinegar, and spice to suit; put all together and simmer till tender. The second day after pour off the syrup and boil down until there will be just enough to cover the melon. Well worth the trouble.

QUINCES, PRESERVED WHOLE.—Pare and put them into a saucepan with the parings at the top; fill with hard water, cover close and set over a gentle fire until they turn a reddish brown. Let them stand till cold, put them into a clear, thick syrup, boil them for a few minutes, set them to one side till quite cold, boil them again in the same manner; the next day boil them until quite clear. If the syrup is not thick enough, boil more; when cold put brandied paper over the fruit. The quinces may be quartered or halved.

PRESERVED PEARS.—Peel, core and cut in halves; weigh one pound of fruit to one pound of sugar. Make a syrup of the sugar, put in some preserved ginger and sliced lemons to flavor it; boil the pears until quite soft, take out into a dish to cool, and boil the syrup ten or fifteen minutes longer.

FRESH PEACHES.—Remove the skins by pouring boiling water on them, a few at a time, and you can peel them like potatoes; weigh them and to each pound of fruit allow a quarter of a pound of sugar, and make a clear syrup, allowing one pound of sugar to one quart of water; put the peaches hot into the jars and fill the jars with hot syrup. If you have not enough syrup add boiling water. The syrup the peaches are boiled in can be used for anything else.

SIBERIAN CRAB-APPLE PRESERVES.—Wipe them, leave the stems on, weigh, and allow one pound of fruit to one pound of sugar; prick the apples with a large needle, which will prevent the skins from cracking; make a syrup of sugar; when clear put in the apples and boil twenty minutes; take them out and lay on a dish to cool; put them into jars and strain the syrup over them.

CITRON MELON PRESERVES. — Peel the melon, take out the inside, and cut it in small pieces, two inches long and one inch wide; put a piece of alum into the water, and boil until the melons are quite tender; then weigh, allowing one pound of sugar to one pound of fruit; drain the melon into a dish, sprinkle the sugar over it and between the pieces, and let it stand over night. The next day pour off the syrup, cut up two lemons into small pieces, removing the seeds, and put them and some preserved ginger into it, and boil till clear; then put the melon in and boil ten or fifteen minutes, take it out on a dish to cool, put into jars and pour the syrup over it. Seal tight.

TO SPICE FRUIT.—For seven pounds of fruit take four pounds of good sugar, one quart of good cider vinegar, cinnamon and cloves tied in a bag.
MRS. S. H——.

BRANDY PEACHES.—To eight pounds of fruit take four pounds of sugar; make a syrup of the sugar, and to every two pints of syrup add one and a half pints of good brandy; cook the peaches until they are heated through; then pour on the syrup and seal air tight. MRS. S. H——.

SPICED GRAPES.—One and a half pounds of sugar, one quart of vinegar, cinnamon and cloves to taste; let it come to a boil; skim it well; put the grapes into a stone jar in bunches; pour the syrup on hot; repeat three or four times.

An excellent rule for canning the larger fruits, peaches, pears &c., is to place them in a steamer over a kettle of boiling water, first laying a cloth in the bottom of the steamer; fill this with the fruit and cover tightly; let them steam for fifteen minutes, or until they can be easily pierced with a fork. Make a syrup of the right consistency; as the fruit is steamed, drop each for a moment into the syrup; then place in the cans, having each half full of fruit; then fill up with the hot fruit syrup; then cover and seal.

LEMON BUTTER.—One and a half cups of white sugar, whites of three eggs, yolk of one egg, grated rind and juice of one and a half lemons; cook, over a slow fire, twenty minutes, stirring all the time.

GRAPE BUTTER.—Pick the grapes from the stems, wash and put them in a kettle with a very little water, as there is a great deal of juice in them; boil till tender, then take off and strain through a colander; put a pound of sugar to a quart of juice, boil, and stir well until done; no spices required. Grapes that fail to ripen may be profitably used in this way.

PRESERVED PEACHES.—Select peaches of fine quality and firm, pare them and place them in a steamer over boiling water and cover tightly; an earthen plate placed in the steamer under the fruit will preserve the juices, which, afterwards, may be strained and added to the syrup; let them steam for fifteen minutes or until they can be easily pierced with a fork. Make a syrup of the best sugar, and, as the fruit is steamed, drop each peach into the syrup for a few seconds then take it out and place in the cans; when the cans are full pour over them the hot syrup and seal immediately. The syrup should be well skimmed before pouring over the fruit; use half or quarter of a pound of sugar to a pound of fruit in canning. This rule is *excellent* for all the large fruits, as pears, quinces, apples &c.

CANNED CHERRIES.—Stone the fruit, weigh it, and to one pound of fruit allow half a pound of best sugar; after putting the fruit into the syrup, let it scald (not boil *hard*) for ten or fifteen minutes, and then can and seal. A few of the cherry stones put in a muslin bag and put into the syrup to scald with the fruit imparts a fine flavor; they should not be put in the jars with the fruit. This method is excellent for use with all the small fruits, as strawberries, raspberries and plums.

CURRANT JELLY.—The currants should be ripe and freshly picked; after the stones are removed place them in a kettle without any water and let them stew gently; remove from the fire when they begin to turn white, and press them through a strainer cloth to extract the juice; to each pint of juice take one pound of white sugar *which has been previously heated* in the oven; then put over the fire and boil fifteen minutes after the sugar has been added; dip it slowly into the jelly glasses, having a wet cloth wrapped around each one to prevent its cracking. Some think a quart of raspberries to a peck of currants is an improvement.

GRAPE JELLY.—Strip from their stems some ripe grapes, and stir with a wooden spoon over a gentle fire until all have burst and the juice flows freely from them; strain through a jelly bag; to every pint of juice put fourteen ounces of sugar; put the juice on to boil fifteen minutes, then add the sugar and boil fifteen minutes longer, keeping it constantly well stirred and skimmed.

CRAB APPLE JELLY.—Put the apples into a kettle with just enough water to cover them; let them boil until they are soft, mash them up and strain through a jelly bag, adding one pound of sugar to one pint of juice; proceed as with other jellies.

QUINCE JELLY.—Take the parings and cores of quinces cover them with water and let them boil two hours; strain, and add one pint of juice to one pound of sugar; proceed as usual

APPLE JELLY.—Boil the apples in a little water, strain through a sieve, and put one pint of juice to one pound of sugar; add the juice of two lemons.

STRAWBERRY, BLACKBERRY OR RASPBERRY JAM—Mash the berries with a wooden spoon, put them into the preserving kettle, and let them cook ten minutes; then add one and a half pounds of sugar to one quart of raw berries

CIDER JELLY.—One and a half ounces of gelatine, the grated rind of one lemon and the juice of three; add one pint of cold water and let it stand one hour; then add two and a half pounds of loaf sugar, three pints of boiling water and one pint of cider. Put into moulds and set in a cool place.

WINE JELLY.—On one box of Coxe's gelatine pour a pint of cold water and let it stand ten minutes; then pour on four pints of boiling water and one pint of wine, and add two pounds of sugar, the juice of three lemons and the grated rind of one. Strain immediately through a jelly bag and let it stand to cool.
MRS. W. S. H———.

ORANGE OR LEMON GELATINE.—Half a box of gelatine dissolved in half a pint of cold water, juice of six and grated rind of one orange, one and a half pints of boiling water and half a cup of sugar. For lemon gelatine after dissolving add one and a half pints of boiling water, one cup of sugar, the juice of three and the rind of one lemon, strain, and set to cool. MRS. W. H———.

APPLE JELLY FOR CAKE.—One large or two small apples grated, the rind and juice of one lemon and one cup of sugar; boil three minutes.

BLACKBERRY CORDIAL. — Heat half a bushel of berries, and express the juice, add two ounces each of allspice, cinnamon and cloves; allow one pound of sugar to a pint of juice; boil thoroughly, and, when cool, add half a gallon of best brandy.

BLACKBERRY CORDIAL, NO. 2—To every quart of juice put one pound of white sugar, half an ounce each of grated nutmeg and cinnamon, and quarter of an ounce each of allspice and cloves, and add one pint of best brandy ; tie the spices in a thin muslin bag; boil juice, sugar and spices together for fifteen minutes, skim well, add the brandy and set aside to cool in a closely covered vessel. When perfectly cold take out the spices, strain and bottle, sealing the corks.

GRAPE WINE. To each quart of grape juice, put two quarts of water and three pounds of sugar. Soak the skins of the grapes in the water.

CURRANT WINE.—Mash and squeeze the currants through a strong cloth. To every two quarts of juice add one quart of water and two pounds loaf sugar. Stir this well and set it away in large stone jars for two or three weeks ; there will be a thick scum ; take this all off and add to every gallon a pint of best brandy or pure spirits. Put it into a demijohn and stop it tight.

QUINCE CORDIAL.—Pare and core the quinces, then grate them; boil them, as well as the parings and cores. Strain, and to two quarts of juice add one pound sugar, one pint brandy, and spices to suit the taste.

CHERRY BOUNCE.—Stone the cherries and put them into a jar; place this jar in a pot of boiling water. Set the pot on the fire and let the water boil around the jar till all the juice is extracted. Strain, and to one gallon of juice add four pounds of sugar, boil and skim, add whole spice, one quart of brandy and one quart of rum.

Sweet Champagne Cider.—Let the cider ferment for two or three weeks; when it is lively add to each gallon one to two pounds sugar, according to the tartness of the cider. Let it work until it has the taste you wish. Then mix for each gallon of cider one fourth ounce of sulphite of lime into one quart of cider, and return it to the rest. In three days it will be clear and ready for you to bottle what will be a sweet, sparkling cider.

Cheap Wine for Cooking.—Take new cider from the press, mix as much honey with it as will support an egg; boil it gently fifteen minutes but *not in iron, brass nor copper*. Skim well and when cool put it into a cask. In the following March it will be ready to bottle—in six weeks ready to drink.

BREAD.

GOOD HOP YEAST.—Take one handful of hops and boil them a minute in a quart of water; then pour the water over six spoonfuls of flour and stir well; let it cool; then stir in a teacupful of good soaked yeast and let it rise well; then stir in corn meal until stiff enough to cut. Keep out in the wind on plates or a clean board till dry.   MRS. S———.

DRIED YEAST. Tin cup of milk-warm water, two cups of fresh butter-milk, two tablespoons of yeast; mix in enough meal to make a thick batter, let it rise in a warm place; then add enough meal to make a stiff dough; roll into thin cakes to dry. Use one tablespoon of dried yeast to one quart of flour. Make up with milk-warm water into loaves of bread, instead of sponge; raise and bake.
    MRS. J. P———.

SALT RISING YEAST.—The night before baking scald one pint of meal, stirring and adding water until it makes a thick gruel; add one tablespoon of sugar, and one teaspoon of salt; keep in a warm place until morning. Then put in one and a half pints of luke warm water, and a small half teaspoonful of soda;

stir in flour enough to make a thick batter; keep in a warm place, raise and knead as in other yeast.

MRS. J. P———.

SALT RISING YEAST, No. 2.—One tablespoon flour, two tablespoons of corn meal; stir to a thick mush with boiling water, cover and set in a warm place over night. In the morning add to one pint of new milk enough boiling water to scald it *slightly*; then pour it over the mush of the previous night; add enough flour to make a thick batter; add a pinch of salt, and the same of sugar. After the sponge is very light and over-flowing mix the dough, adding a little warm water if needed, and work very *thoroughly* before setting to rise.

MRS. G. L———.

EXCELLENT LIGHT BREAD. — Soak two tablespoonfuls of dry hop yeast (or half a cake compressed yeast,) for an hour, in enough warm water to cover it. Then, with flour and a little additional warm water, make about a quart of batter. Let it rise over night; in the summer set it in a cool place, in the winter, near the fire. In the morning sift about as much flour as the batter *and* a pint of warm water will mix, add salt, and if desirable a little lard; knead until perfectly smooth. *In fifteen or twenty minutes* knead again, *diligently*. Let it rise until *quite* light, then knead again *well*; let it stand a few minutes *only*, then knead again into *small* loaves. Do not grease the pan, but always grease each loaf well with sweet lard or butter. Bake in a slow oven; when thoroughly done, take out the pan, grease the loaves over the top with a little butter, cover them *while in the pan*, with a piece of thick paper. After remaining in the pan fifteen minutes, take the loaves out and let them remain a few minutes, right side up. *When* perfectly *cold* put away in a tin box, or as convenient. For light rolls—take off a piece of dough after the second kneading, add a little more lard, and bake as directed for the loaves.

MRS. JUDGE T———.

VIENNA ROLLS.—To one quart of flour add two teaspoons of best baking powder; sift thoroughly, add a little salt, and rub a tablespoonful of lard or butter through the flour; use enough sweet milk to make a soft dough; roll out, and cut with a round cutter; fold over like a turn-over, and wet the edges with milk, to make them adhere; wash over with milk to give them a gloss. Place in a pan so that they will not touch; bake fifteen or twenty minutes.

MRS. H. M———.

PARKER HOUSE ROLLS.—Two quarts of flour, one tablespoon of lard, one teaspoon of salt; rub well together; scald one pint of milk; when cool, mix with the milk half a teacup of hop yeast and half a cup of white sugar; make a hole in the flour and pour in the mixture; stir it around with enough of the flour to make a sponge; cover it and set it in a warm place to rise; when light, mould into rather a stiff dough; let it rise again; roll it out an inch thick, cut it into strips an inch wide and three inches long and lay them on buttered tins; when light, bake in a quick oven.

Soda Biscuits.—One quart of flour, one heaping tablespoon of lard, one pint of milk (nearly), one teaspoon of soda, scraped off with a knife, two small teaspoons of cream of tartar; sift soda and cream of tartar thoroughly in the flour, then rub in the lard and add a little salt. Pour in enough milk to make a soft dough and mix quickly; roll out half an inch thick, and bake in a quick oven.

Steamed Brown Bread.—Three teacups Graham flour, four teacups of corn meal, one cup of molasses, one teaspoon of soda, one teaspoon of salt, one quart of buttermilk, one tablespoon of brown sugar; steam six hours.

Brown Bread.—Two coffee cups of Indian meal, one cup of molasses, one quart sweet milk, one teaspoon of salt, two teaspoons of baking powder, two eggs; stir with flour about as stiff as for cake, and bake in a pudding dish; or it can be steamed two or three hours, and then set in the oven to brown.

Graham Bread.—It is a good plan to take a certain quantity of the risen sponge on baking day and set it aside for brown bread. Put into a pan two parts Graham flour, and one part white flour, and to every quart of this add a handful of Indian meal and a teaspoon of salt: wet this up with the sponge, and, for a fair sized loaf, add one half cup molasses. The dough should be very soft and handled as little as possible; add warm water, if you have not enough sponge to make it of the proper consistency. Bake slowly. Give it time to rise and to bake. Do not cut while hot. Most persons prefer not to sift brown flour.

CREAM BISCUITS.—Three heaping teaspoons of baking powder in a quart of flour which has been sifted three times, a lump of butter the size of a walnut, a pinch of salt, and one half pint of cream. Mix daintily with tips of fingers. Roll out thin, and bake a delicate brown.

FLANNEL ROLLS.—One cup of sweet milk, whites of two eggs, two thirds of a cup of butter, flour to make a thick batter, two tablespoons of sugar and two teaspoons baking powder. Form into rolls, let them rise—then bake.

RUSK.—To one tumbler of milk put one half gill of yeast, three eggs, one half cup of sugar, butter size of an egg and a little nutmeg or lemon. Melt the butter, pour it into the milk warm, add the yeast, sugar, the well beaten eggs, and flour enough to make a dough. Let it rise over night; when very light roll out and put it on tins to rise again.

BUNNS.—One quart of flour, one pint of warm milk, four tablespoons of butter, and one gill of yeast. Mix them and set it to rise three or four hours. Then add two beaten eggs and one fourth pound of sugar. Mix this into the dough and set it to rise about two hours. When very light make the dough into bunns, and set them close together to rise. When all of a sponge brush the top with a little milk and molasses mixed. Set in a quick oven and bake fifteen or twenty minutes.

LUNCHEON CAKE.—One pound of dough, two ounces of butter, two ounces of powdered sugar and two eggs. Beat all well together in a basin, using the hand instead of an egg-beater. Set it in a plain mould to rise for three quarters of an hour, then bake in a quick oven. When eaten it should have the appearance of honeycomb. This is nice luncheon cake, and will make delicious toast when stale.

BAKING POWDER BISCUITS.—One quart of flour, two teaspoons of baking powder, a little salt, lard the size of an egg, and enough sweet milk to mix into a soft dough. MRS. J. H. M——.

BAKING POWDER BISCUITS, No. 2.—One quart of flour, sifted two or three times, two heaping teaspoons of baking powder, a pinch of salt, and one tablespoon of lard *mixed thoroughly* through the flour. Then pour in one half pint of cream, (or cream and water) do not knead much, but roll out on the board; double the dough and roll again, repeating this once or twice. Do not touch the hands to it any more than necessary; cut into biscuits; *make them* touch each other in the pan. You will have delicious biscuits with very little trouble.

MRS. W. W. B ——.

CORN BREAD.—One pint of sour milk, two cups of meal, one cup of flour, half a cup of molasses, a teaspoonful of soda and a little salt; steam two hours; bake one hour. MRS. M. P. J——.

CORN BREAD, No. 2.—Four cups of corn meal, two cups of rye flour, three cups of sour milk, one cup of molasses, one teaspoon of soda, salt. Steam three hours and bake half an hour.

MRS. M. P. J——.

Graham Gems.—One cup Graham flour, one half cup of white flour, one tablespoon of butter, one egg, one tablespoon of sugar, a little salt, three large tablespoons of baking powder, enough milk to make a stiff batter; heat the tins : add the eggs last.

MRS. M. P. J——.

Cream Puffs.—Heat one fourth pound of butter; add one half pint of sweet milk and let it come to a boil; then add by degrees six ounces of flour, and stir *it well while on the stove*, until the dough looks very smooth and dark. Empty it into a bowl and stir in (without beating) five eggs; have a hot oven ; drop little balls into lightly greased pans and bake them; when they have risen high, and baked a nice brown, they are done: take very thick cream and whip it stiff, sweeten well with powdered sugar, and flavor with vanilla; open the puffs just a little on the side and fill them.

MRS. S. H——.

Crumb Cakes.—To one pint of sour milk put one cup of bread crumbs, a little salt, two well beaten eggs, and flour enough to make a batter, not too stiff; add a small flat-teaspoonful of soda just before baking. Bake as buckwheat cakes.

Buckwheat Cakes.—One quart of warm water, one large spoonful of Indian meal, scalded, one teaspoon of salt, four tablespoons of yeast and one large spoonful of molasses ; stir in enough buckwheat flour to make a thin batter. Let it rise over night and, in the morning, add a pinch of soda. They should be as thin as will turn over, and no more grease used than needed to keep them from sticking.

BREAD.

FLANNEL CAKES.—Mix three tablespoons of flour with half of a pint of cream, add two eggs, and beat the whole very smooth. Then add slowly one half pint new milk into which has been put a teaspoon of baking powder. Beat well together and fry in hot lard. Eat with powdered sugar mixed with grated nutmeg or cinnamon.

BREAKFAST CAKES.—One pint of sour milk with one scant teaspoon of soda stirred in it until it foams like soda water; the well beaten yolks of two or three eggs, a little salt, and flour enough to make a batter, not too thick; lastly add the beaten whites; bake in plenty of hot lard, on a moderately hot griddle.

MRS. W. W. B——.

For corn meal cakes use meal instead of flour. Do not use as hot a griddle as for flour cakes.

VERY PLAIN CORN BREAD.—One pint of corn meal, with a little salt and a teaspoon of lard stirred in; wet with enough water to make a very thick batter; bake on a griddle. MRS. B——.

KENTUCKY BISCUIT.—One quart of flour, two tablespoons of lard, one teaspoon of salt; make up stiff with water and beat with a potato masher, for fifteen minutes. Bake in a quick oven.

GRAHAM GEMS, No 2.—One cup of sour milk, one teaspoon of soda, one teaspoon of salt, half of a cup of molasses, Graham flour enough to make a stiff batter; stir hard and bake in muffin irons.

POP OVERS.—One cup of flour, one cup of sweet milk, one egg, and a pinch of salt; beat thoroughly; heat the pans and butter them; fill half full with the batter, and bake in a quick oven.

CAKES.

COFFEE CAKE.—Four eggs, two cups of brown sugar, one cup of butter, one cup of molasses, one cup of cold coffee, one half pound of raisins, one half nutmeg, two teaspoons of cloves, one teaspoon of soda, and four cups of flour.

SPONGE CAKE.—Three eggs, one cup sugar, one cup of flour, two tablespoons of sweet milk, and one teaspoon of baking powder.

MRS. J. H. M——.

SPONGE CAKE, No. 2.—Two eggs, one cup of sugar, five tablespoons of water, one and a half cups of flour, one and a half teaspoons of baking powder. For jelly cake, bake in layers.

SPONGE ROLL, No. 3.—Three eggs, one cup of sugar, one half cup of sweet milk, one cup of flour, one and a half teaspoons of baking powder; pour it *thin* into a baking pan, bake slowly and when done spread jelly or jam over it, roll up and wrap it in a cloth.

SPONGE CAKE, No. 4.—One coffee cup of sugar, same of flour, five eggs, one lemon, one teaspoon of baking powder or not. Nice.

MRS. M. P. J——.

CAKES. 83

Sponge Cake, No. 5.—Twelve eggs leaving out the yolks of two; eighteen ounces of sugar, twelve ounces of flour, one lemon; heat the flour.

MRS. M. P. J——.

Cream Sponge Cake, No. 6.—Six eggs, one pint of flour *and* one tablespoonful extra, one half teacup of ice water *added last;* two teaspoons of baking powder. *For the cream*—Three fourths pint of rich cream, two tablespoons of sugar, two teaspoons of corn starch; let it come to a boil; when cold, spread between the layers.

MRS. C. W. L——.

Sponge Cake, No. 7. — Two eggs, thoroughly beaten with one cup of sugar, one third cup of boiling water; sift two teaspoons of baking powder into an even teacup of sifted flour; season with lemon or vanilla. By the use of one more egg you can make any kind of layer cake, better than with the butter in: for *this*, save the two whites for the frosting, using two yolks and one egg for the cake. Bake in jelly tins. If desired sprinkle *cocoanut* over each layer of frosting; or, for *chocolate,* use one half teacup Baker's chocolate grated and stirred into the frosting.

Seal Brown Cake.—The whites of seven eggs, two cups of sugar, one cup of milk, one cup of butter, two and a half cups of flour, one and a half cups of grated chocolate, two teaspoons of baking powder, one teaspoon of vanilla; bake in jelly pans, and put together with chocolate paste, made as follows: two cups of grated chocolate, one cup of water, eight tablespoons of sugar, one tablespoon of butter; boil to a thick paste.

WHITE MOUNTAIN CAKE.—Whites of six eggs, two thirds of a cup of butter, one cup sweet milk, two cups of sugar, three cups of flour, two teaspoons of baking powder.

FRUIT CAKE.—One pound of butter, one pound of sugar, one pound of flour, ten eggs, two pounds of currants, two pounds of raisins, one pound of citron, one wineglass of brandy, two nutmegs, one large tablespoon of molasses, one teaspoon *each* of cinnamon, cloves and allspice.

SNOW CAKE.—Whites of ten eggs, one and a half tumblers of powdered sugar, one tumbler of flour, one teaspoon of cream tartar; flavor to taste.

COFFEE CAKE, No. 2.—Two teacups of sugar, one teacup of butter, two thirds of a cup of molasses, one cup of strong coffee, four eggs, four cups of flour, one tablespoon each of cloves and cinnamon, one nutmeg, one teaspoon of soda, one cup of raisins, a cup of currants, half a cup of citron.

ICE-CREAM CAKE.—Take the whites of five eggs, one and a half cups of sugar, half a cup of butter, a cup of milk, one and a half teaspoons of baking powder, three cups of flour. Separate this mixture and color half of it with strawberry coloring. Flavor *this* with vanilla; the white with lemon. Put in the white, then the pink, and so on. Bake slowly.

ICE-CREAM CAKE, No. 2.—Two cups of sugar, one cup of butter, three cups flour, a half cup of sweet milk, the whites of eight eggs, two teaspoons of baking powder. Bake in layers.

Cream for the above.—Two and one half cups of sugar, with enough water to moisten it thoroughly; then boil. Beat the whites of three eggs to a stiff froth, and when the syrup is clear pour it on them hot, and stir fast; add one teaspoon of citric acid; flavor with vanilla.

MISS M. E. C———.

COCOANUT ROSE CAKE.—Cream half a cup of butter with one and a half cups of sugar. Dissolve a scant teaspoon of soda in two teaspoons of boiling water, and add to it half a cup of thick, sweet cream. Whip the cream to a froth, and mix it lightly with the butter and sugar. Then add two teaspoons of cream tartar, sifted through two and a half cups of flour; add *finally* the whites of five eggs, beaten to a stiff froth. Flavor with vanilla, and color a light pink, with cochineal or analine; a drop or two will color the whole cake.

Cocoanut Filling.—Beat the whites of two eggs to a stiff froth; add one cup of powdered sugar and two thirds of a grated cocoanut. Put this between the layers and cover the top with a portion, over which sprinkle the balance of the cocoanut, mixed with a little powdered sugar.

M. E. C———.

ALMOND CAKE.—Three cups of sugar, one cup of butter, one cup of sweet milk, the whites of twelve eggs beaten to a stiff froth; five cups of flour, three teaspoons of baking powder sifted with the flour. Flavor with lemon.

Icing for this Cake.—The whites of four eggs beaten to a stiff froth, one pound of pulverized sugar, half a tablespoon of cream tartar, half a tablespoon of corn starch and two pounds of chopped almonds mixed with the icing and spread between the layers.

M. E. C——.

Fig Cake.—The whites of six eggs, two cups of white sugar, two cups of flour, one cup of corn starch, one cup of milk, one and a third cups of butter, one and a half teaspoons of baking powder; flavor to taste; bake in four layers. *Dark Part.*—Yolks of six eggs, one cup of brown sugar, half a teaspoon of soda dissolved in half a cup of water, half a cup of butter, half a nutmeg, one teaspoon of cinnamon, *nearly* two cups of flour, one and a half cups of chopped raisins, half a pound of figs chopped fine; mix the figs and raisins with the flour. Bake in three layers. Put the layers together with icing.

MRS. J. H. M——.

Fig Cake, No. 2.—Make any white cake and bake it in five layers. Take a pound of figs, chop them fine, put in a pan with one cup of sugar and a pint of water. Let it stew slowly, on the back of the stove an hour and a half, stirring frequently. This should become a thick paste; then spread it between the layers.

MRS. C. V. J——.

White Mountain Cake, No. 2.—Three cups of sugar, a cup of butter, half a cup of sweet milk, the whites of ten eggs, three teaspoons baking powder, sifted into four and a half cups of flour; flavor with vanilla. Bake in layers. Put icing between, made of the whites of three eggs, and one pound of powdered sugar.

WHITE CAKE, No. 1.— The whites of twelve eggs, three cups of flour, two cups of sugar, a cup of butter, two teaspoons of baking powder. Beat the eggs and sugar together very light, and cream the flour in the butter.

WHITE CAKE, No. 2.—The whites of eight eggs, well beaten, two teacups white sugar, two thirds cup of butter, three cups flour, one cup sweet milk, two teaspoons baking powder, mixed with the flour; flavor.

To make cocoanut, chocolate, or any other kind of cake of this, bake your cake in a mould, same as if you wished a plain cake of it; when cold, turn the cake bottom side up and slice in layers from the bottom around the cake, then put whatever you wish between the layers, putting your cake *together* as you cut it apart. When done ice it over and you have a pretty cake.

MRS. J. H. M——.

WHITE CAKE, No. 3.—Three cups sugar, one cup butter, one cup sweet milk, four and three-fourths cups flour, six teaspoons best baking powder, the whites of twelve eggs. Flavor with lemon.

MRS. WM. H——.

WHITE CAKE, No. 4.—Three cups sugar, one cup butter, one cup sweet milk, five cups flour, twelve eggs, (whites) two teaspoons baking powder.

MRS. S. S. L——.

CARAMEL CAKE.—Make a cake after the above recipe for white cake, and bake it in jelly tins. *Caramel for filling.*—One and a half tea cups of brown sugar, a half tea cup of sweet milk, a tea cup of molasses, a teaspoon of butter, a tablespoon of flour, two tablespoons of cold water. Boil this mixture and add half a teacup of Baker's chocolate. Boil till thick as custard and add a pinch of soda: flavor with lemon.

GOLD CAKE, No. 1.—The yolks of eight eggs, one and a half cups of sugar, half a cup of butter, half a cup of milk and water, two cups of flour, two teaspoons of baking powder.

SILVER CAKE, No. 1.—The whites of eight eggs, two cups of powdered sugar, half a cup of butter, half a cup of sweet milk, three cups of flour, one and a half teaspoons of baking powder.

MRS. M. P. J——.

SNOW CAKE, No. 1.—One and a half cups of sugar, one cup of flour, the whites of ten eggs, two teaspoons of baking powder. Flavor.

MRS. CONNELLY'S CREAM CAKE.—Ten eggs, their weight in sugar, and one half their weight in flour. Beat the eggs separately. Beat the sugar in the yolks, then the whites, and, lastly, add the flour, a little at a time. Bake in a biscuit pan—split in two and spread cream between, made as follows:—one half pint of milk, two small teaspoons of corn starch, one egg, one teaspoonful of vanilla and half a cup of sugar. Heat the milk to boiling and stir in the corn starch, previously mixed with a little cold milk; take out a little and mix it gradually with the beaten egg and sugar. Return this to the rest of the custard, and boil, *stirring constantly*, until quite thick. Let it cool before you flavor it, and then spread it between the layers.

CREAM CAKE, NO. 2—Two eggs, one cup of sugar, one cup of flour, one teaspoon of cream tartar, one half teaspoon of soda, in a large teaspoonful of milk. Flavor with lemon. *Cream.*—One half pint of milk, two tablespoons of sugar, one tablespoon of corn starch, one egg. Scald the milk, stir in the eggs and corn starch, after the sugar has been put in. Bake the cake in layers and spread the cream between.

MRS. W. H———.

DOLLY VARDEN CAKE.—Two cups of sugar, one third cup of butter, one cup of sweet milk, three teaspoons of baking powder, three cups of flour, three eggs. Bake one half of this in jelly tins. To the other half put one half cup of chopped raisins, one cup of currants, one teaspoon of molasses and one teaspoon of each spice, except cloves. Put frosting between. Flavor with lemon.

MRS. W. S. H———.

DOLLY VARDEN CAKE, NO. 2.—*Dark part.* One cup sugar, half a cup butter, half a cup syrup, two thirds cup sweet milk, two cups flour, yolks of four eggs, two teaspoons baking powder, one cup chopped raisins, half a cup chopped figs, one teaspoon of cinnamon and half a teaspoon of cloves.

Light part.—The whites of three eggs, one cup of sweet milk, one and a half cups of sugar, half a cup of butter, two cups of flour, two teaspoons of baking powder and two teaspoons of vanilla; bake in square tins, and put together in alternate layers with jelly between. Make a frosting for the top with the remaining whites and the sugar.

CUSTARD CAKE.—One cup of flour; one cup of sugar, three eggs, two tablespoons of sweet milk and two teaspoons of baking powder. Bake in jelly tins, and spread with cream made as follows: one pint of sweet milk, half a cup of butter, two thirds of a cup of sugar. When this boils, stir in two well-beaten eggs, two tablespoons of corn starch, previously mixed with cold milk, and flavor with lemon.

RIBBON CAKE.—Two cups of butter, four cups of sugar, two cups of sour cream, seven cups of flour, nine eggs, and two teaspoons of baking powder.

BOSTON POUND CAKE.—One pound of sugar, three fourths of a pound of butter, one pound of flour, six eggs, one cup of cream or rich milk, one teaspoon of baking powder and two grated lemons. Beat the butter and sugar to a cream, to which add, gradually, the cream and lemon with a fourth part of the flour. Whisk the eggs until thick, (do not separate), and stir in one third at a time. After mixing well add the remaining flour; beat all well together, ten or fifteen minutes, and stir in the baking powder thoroughly, without much beating. Butter the pan, put in the batter, spread over smooth with a knife, and bake in a moderate oven.

MRS. S. H——.

FRUIT CAKE.—Three fourths of a pound each of butter, sugar and flour, eight eggs, a gill of cream, one teaspoon of cinnamon and nutmeg mixed, half a gill of brandy, a pound of currants, *washed, dried* and *picked* and a pound of raisins seeded and chopped. Beat the butter, sugar and spices until very light, then add the cream and a fourth part of the flour. Whisk the eggs until thick, which add by degrees. Then add the remainder of the flour, half at a time, lastly the fruit. Beat all well together. Butter the pan and line it with white paper, and bake the cake in a moderate oven.

MRS. S. H——.

JAMTIFTIGE TARTE.—Ten eggs, beaten separately, one and a half cups of sugar, the grated rind of two lemons, one teaspoon of ground cinnamon, one teaspoon of cloves, half a teaspoon of allspice, one fourth of a teaspoon of grated almonds, one saucer of raisins, five cents worth of citron, one saucer of grated bread soaked in brandy, four grated apples.

MRS. S. H——.

DELICATE CAKE.—The whites of sixteen eggs, two teacups of the best sugar, half a cup of butter, three cups of flour and one teaspoon of baking powder. Heat the flour in the oven, but do not brown it.

MRS. M. P. J——.

FEATHER CAKE.—Half a cup of butter, one cup of sugar, half a cup of sweet milk, one and a half cups of flour, one egg and two teaspoons of baking powder.

MRS. M. P. J———.

LOAF CAKE.—One cup of molasses, one cup of brown sugar, one cup of butter, one cup of sour milk, four cups of flour, one teaspoon of cloves, half a pound each of raisins and currants, one fourth of a pound of citron, a little salt and a teaspoon of soda dissolved in a little warm water.

MRS. M. P. J———.

BLACK CAKE.—Two cups brown sugar, one cup molasses, one and a half cups butter, yolks of four eggs, or three whole eggs, two thirds of a cup of boiling water and two teaspoons of soda; raisins, currants, citron and spices to taste. Make a very stiff batter.

MRS. M. P. J———.

AUNT ANGIE'S BLACK OR FRUIT CAKE.—One pound of sugar, one pound of dark browned flour, three fourths of a pound of butter, twelve eggs, one pint of dark molasses, one glass of wine, one large wineglass of brandy, one tablespoon of ground cinnamon, one teaspoon of ground cloves, one teaspoon of mace, two nutmegs, two pounds of raisins, two pounds of currants, half a pound of citron, two teaspoons of baking powder and a pinch of black pepper; dredge the fruit in flour, and put it in last. Beat the butter and sugar together, then put in the eggs and molasses, then brandy, wine, spices, the flour in which the baking powder has been sifted, and, lastly, the fruit. Make into one large cake, and bake from two to three hours. Brown the flour in the oven until *quite* brown, and use the darkest sugar you can find. The whites and yolks are beaten together.

MRS. W. H———.

CURRANT CAKE.—The yolks of eight eggs, two cups of sugar, one cup of butter, one cup of sweet milk, four cups of flour, two teaspoons of baking powder and one teaspoon of cinnamon. Add one pound of currants with the last cup of flour.

MRS. S. S. L———.

CORN STARCH CAKE.—Two cups of sugar, one cup of butter, one cup of milk, two cups of flour, half a cup of corn starch, three eggs and one and a half teaspoons of baking powder. Sift the starch with the flour.

VELVET CAKE. Two cups of sugar, three cups of flour, half a cup of butter, four eggs, one teacup of cold water, two teaspoons of baking powder; flavor with lemon. Beat the butter and sugar to a cream, sift the powder with the flour, then gradually add the flour and the water to the butter and sugar; beat the eggs separately; add them and then beat all well together.

PLUM CAKE.—One cup of butter, three cups of sugar, three and a half cups of flour, one pound of raisins, one pound of currants (or figs chopped fine) one tablespoon of cinnamon, half a nutmeg, half a pound of citron, sliced very thin, three eggs, well beaten together, one cup of sweet milk and four teaspoons of baking powder; flavor to suit the taste. This can be used for steamed pudding.

ORANGE CAKE.— Mix *well* together the yolks (without beating) of two eggs, and two cups of sugar, then add the *beaten* whites.—Next add a large spoonful of butter, a cup of sweet milk, three cups of flour and two teaspoons of baking powder; flavor and bake in jelly tins. *Filling.*—Grate the rinds of two oranges and a lemon, add the juice of the same and one cup of water, one cup of sugar and a tablespoon of corn starch; boil, and cool before using.

ORANGE CAKE, No. 2.—Two cups of sugar and the yolks of five eggs beaten to a cream, the whites of four eggs, five tablespoons of cold water, two cups of flour mixed well with three teaspoons of baking powder, and the juice of one lemon; add the beaten whites last. *Between.*—The whites of two eggs, the rind of one and the juice of two medium sized oranges, and one pint of pulverized sugar. Bake the cake in two large jelly tins; when done split with a very sharp knife, and put the mixture between.

MRS. G. S. B——.

HICKORY NUT CAKE.—Two cups of sugar, three fourths of a cup of butter, three cups of flour, three teaspoons of baking powder, mixed well with the flour, three fourths of a cup of sweet milk, the whites of six eggs, one pint of nuts and one cup of seeded and chopped raisins well floured.

MRS. G. S. B——.

COCOANUT CAKE.—Five eggs beaten separately, two cups of white sugar, one cup of butter, and four cups of flour into which two teaspoons of baking powder have been well sifted. Add the flour to the butter, sugar, and eggs, by degrees, after they have been well beaten, with one cup of new milk. Flavor with lemon or vanilla; bake in jelly cake pans. Get a box of desiccated cocoanut, beat the whites of three eggs with one cup of sugar, spread the icing on, and sprinkle with cocoanut. Spread it between the layers and on the top.

ANGEL CAKE.—One and a half tumblers of granulated sugar, the whites of eleven eggs, one tumbler of flour, one teaspoon of cream tartar. Beat the whites of the eggs to a stiff froth, into which stir the sugar, after it has been sifted five times; sift the flour, with the cream tartar in it, five times, and stir very lightly into the eggs and sugar. Flavor with vanilla and bake in a gallon milk pan, in a slow oven, forty minutes.

MRS. C. V. J——.

ICING

THE whites of four eggs, one pound of powdered sugar, half a tablespoon each of cream tartar and corn starch; flavoring to suit the taste.

MRS. S. S. L——.

BOILED ICING.—Boil one pound of loaf sugar, with a very little water, to a clear, thick syrup, then pour it slowly into the whites of four eggs well beaten; stir briskly until cool; add a little vinegar, and flavor to taste.

LEMON PASTE.—Grate two lemons, add the juice, one cup of white sugar, one large spoonful of butter and the yolks of three eggs; stir constantly over the fire until it jellies; when cold spread between the cakes.

SMALL CAKES AND COOKIES.

BERRY SHORT CAKE.—One quart of sifted flour, one fourth of a pound of butter, or butter and suet together, chopped fine in the flour, two heaping teaspoons of white sugar, two teaspoons baking powder, all wet with cold water or milk to the right consistency, and rolled quite thin, as for jelly cake. Bake in sheets, in a quick oven, till just done, without browning. Then spread fruit of any kind twice the thickness of the layers, alternating fruit and layers until the whole is as thick as desired. Strawberries should be mashed an hour before using, and well sprinkled with sugar. Return to the oven with the fruit, and brown the sides and top. Serve with cream. Apple jam or sauce, canned peaches mashed, rich rhubarb sauce, or *best lemon paste* can be substituted for berries.

RICH COOKIES, No. 1.—Four teacups flour, one teacup butter, one and a half teacups sugar, two eggs and half a teaspoon soda dissolved in water. Roll thin.

MRS. S. S. L——.

COOKIES, No. 2.—One and a half cups of sugar, three fourths of a cup of butter, three eggs, two tablespoons of water, one teaspoon of baking powder; flavor, and mix stiff enough to roll nicely.

MRS. J. H. M——.

SCOTCH COOKIES, No. 3.—One and a half cups of sugar, half a cup of molasses, one and a fourth cups of butter and lard, two eggs, one teaspoon of soda, one teaspoon of cloves, one teaspoon of allspice and two teaspoons of cinnamon; flavor to taste, roll out thin, and bake.

MOLASSES COOKIES, No. 4.—Two cups molasses, one cup brown sugar, one cup butter, three-fourths cup boiling water, two heaping teaspoons of soda —flour to roll out.

MRS. M. P. J——.

COOKIES, No. 5.—Two cups sugar, one cup butter, one cup sour milk or water, one teaspoon of soda, and a little nutmeg. Do not make dough too stiff; use barely enough flour to keep it from sticking to the moulding board. Roll thin.

MRS. WM. H——.

GINGER CAKES.—One pint of molasses, one teacup of sugar, one teacup of butter or lard, one teacup of warm water, one tablespoon of ginger, one teaspoon of cinnamon, one tablespoon of soda and one teaspoon of pulverized alum. Roll thin.

MRS. S. S. L——.

GINGER SNAPS.—Two cups of molasses, nine teaspoons of melted butter, three teaspoons of ginger, one teaspoon of soda dissolved in hot water, enough flour to stiffen, and roll thin.

SMALL CAKES AND COOKIES.

GINGER SNAPS, No. 2.—One cup sugar, one cup molasses, one cup butter, two eggs, two teaspoons baking powder, one tablespoon ginger; mix stiff enough to roll nicely.

MRS. J. H. M———.

FRENCH DOUGHNUTS.—One cup of butter, three cups of white sugar, one pint of sweet milk, with two teaspoons of cream tartar dissolved in it, four eggs, one teaspoon of soda sifted in three pints of flour, and the juice of one lemon.

MRS. GEO. B———.

SCOTCH CAKES.—Two and a half pounds of sugar, one and a fourth pounds of butter, three pounds of flour, five eggs, half a pint of molasses, one ounce soda mixed with the molasses. Roll very thin, brush over when rolled with a well beaten egg, cut with cake cutter, bake in a quick oven, giving each cake *plenty* of room.

MRS. G. S. B———.

DOUGHNUTS.—One cup of sugar, one egg, a small tablespoon of butter, a scant cup of milk, flour enough to make stiff, in which is mixed two teaspoons of baking powder.

MRS. C. V. J———.

JUMBLES.—One heaping coffee cup of sugar, one *even* cup of butter, four eggs, one fourth of a teaspoon of soda, dissolved in a little warm water. Flour to roll soft and very thin.

MRS. M. P. J———.

JUMBLES, No. 2.—Two cups of sugar, one cup each of butter and sweet milk, three eggs and two teaspoons of baking powder. Mix the butter and sugar, then the yolks, add the milk, whites and flour enough to drop in pans, lastly the baking powder. Sprinkle on a little sugar and cinnamon before baking.

SUGAR DROPS.—Six teaspoons of butter, twelve teaspoons of sugar, (heat the butter) six eggs, half a cup of cold water and flour enough to make a stiff batter. Drop with a teaspoon and bake.

LADY FINGERS. — Four eggs beaten separately very light, three ounces sugar, three ounces flour. Beat the yolks and sugar together, put in the flour and flavoring, and stir all well together. Drop through a funnel, sift on sugar and then bake moderately.

DROP CAKES.—Four eggs, one pint milk, a little salt, flour enough to make a batter, not stiff. Bake in cups.

BACHELORS' BUTTONS.—Rub two ounces butter in five ounces of flour, add five ounces of sugar. Beat one egg with half of the sugar, then put it to the other ingredients; add flavoring to taste. Roll them in the hand, size of a large nut, sprinkle with sugar, place on tins with buttered paper, and bake lightly.

SAND TARTS.—One cup sugar, half a cup of butter, one egg, a pinch of soda dissolved in hot water, cinnamon, and flour enough to roll out thin.

MRS. S. H———.

MACCAROONS.—One pound sugar, half a pound grated almonds, one ounce bitter almonds, and the whites of seven eggs. Mix the almonds, blanched and pounded quite fine; beat the eggs very stiff, then add the sugar, a teaspoonful at a time, until all is added, stir in the almonds lightly. Put on white paper with a teaspoon, about an inch apart, and bake in a cool oven.

PUDDINGS.

LEMON PUDDING.—Half a pound of butter, half a pound of sugar, two ounces of stale sponge cake, rubbed fine, five eggs, two tablespoons of rose water and brandy mixed, and the juice and grated rind of one lemon. Beat the butter and sugar very light, then add the grated sponge cake; whisk the eggs until very light, which stir in by degrees, lastly the brandy, rose water and lemon, alternately. Mix well without beating too much. This will make two puddings, soup plate size. Line your dish with a rich paste, and bake in a quick oven. When done, sift sugar over it.
MRS. S. H——.

LEMON CUSTARD.—The grated rind and juice of two lemons, half a cup of butter, three cups of sugar, six eggs, one quart of milk. Stir the sugar and butter, then the yolks; beat the whites and stir them in. Bake in a buttered dish.
MRS. S. H——.

SUET PUDDING.—One cup chopped suet, one cup raisins, one cup molasses, one cup sweet milk, one teaspoon soda, and flour enough to make a batter; steam three hours. To be eaten with sauce.
MRS. M. P. J——.

Fig Pudding, No. 1.—Six ounces bread crumbs six ounces suet, six ounces sugar, half a pound of figs chopped fine, three eggs, one cup milk, half a glass of brandy, or not, one nutmeg and two teaspoons of baking powder. Steam three hours.

Mrs. M. P. J――――.

Suet Pudding, No. 2.—One cup suet chopped fine, one cup brown sugar, one cup milk, one cup raisins, two and a half cups flour, three teaspoons of baking powder. Mix, and boil in a pudding mould, or floured bag, two and a half hours.

Mrs. C. V. J―――― & Mrs. K. R――――.

Danish Pudding.—Eight eggs, one quart of milk, two tablespoons of sugar, one tablespoon of vanilla, a pinch of salt and two cups of sugar, browned nicely. Have cake in another pan of boiling water. Serve cold.

Mrs. K. R――――.

Snow Pudding.—Dissolve half a box of Coxe's gelatine in a pint of boiling water; add the juice of three lemons; sweeten to taste, and let it cool; when nearly cold add the whites of three eggs beaten stiff, then pour into a mould, to cool. When ready to serve, whip cream, sweeten it a little, and pour it over the pudding.

Mrs. M. P. J――――.

Double-quick Pudding.—One egg, one cup sugar, one cup flour, half a cup cream, half a cup raisins, two teaspoons butter, two teaspoons baking powder, stirred in the flour; stir all together, and steam or bake. *Sauce for same.*—Three heaping tablespoons of sugar, one of flour, two of butter; stir until smooth. Pour on boiling water until it is of the consistency of cream; boil it one minute; flavor with vanilla.

MRS. J. C. J———.

COTTAGE PUDDING.—One cup sugar, two eggs beaten together very light, three tablespoons melted butter, one teacup sweet milk, one pint flour and two teaspoons baking powder. Flavor.

APPLE BATTER PUDDING.—Peel six tart baking apples, core them, and fill the cavities with sugar; put them in a deep dish, and cover with batter. If the apples have been previously baked until quite done, sponge cake batter poured over the apples makes a nice pudding. To be eaten hot with cream or sauce.

APPLES A-LA TURQUE.—Pare and core a dozen good apples, put them into a basin with some thin syrup and the yellow rind of a lemon; cover closely, and simmer until they are soft and clear. Take them out and lay them on a dish with wet white paper over them; this will prevent them from discoloring. Now cover a dish with puff paste, prick the bottom and bake it. When the paste is done fill the holes made by the removal of the cores of the apples with raspberry jam, and arrange them on the paste in the shape of a cone. Beat the whites of six eggs to a stiff snow, and add to them six ounces of white sugar. Mix this gently, and pile the meringue mass upon the apples. Sift a little white sugar over it, and set it into the oven until it is of a light brown color.

POTATO PUDDING.—Pare six good sized potatoes, place them in a chopping bowl, scatter over them enough flour to fill a teacup, add salt, pepper and butter to taste, chop fine and mix well. Grease a deep pie tin, spread the mixture in it and cover with cream. Bake slowly half or three quarters of an hour.

BOMBAY PUDDING.—To a good, sweet custard add a little butter, grated nutmeg and a glass of wine or brandy. Have ready a nicely grated cocoanut and mix all well together. Line your dish with puff paste. Pour in the custard and bake a light brown. It is nice without the crust.

BREAD AND BUTTER PUDDING. — Take half a pound of bread, cut in slices, and spread it thick with butter. Take a deep pudding dish well buttered; cover the bottom with slices of the bread, strew in a few currants, stoned raisins or even jam,—then another layer of bread, and so on. Make a custard of one and a half pints of milk, four or five eggs, half a cup of sugar, a little nutmeg and salt, and a pinch of soda. Pour this over the bread; let it stand two hours; bake one hour.

BUNN PUDDING. Take as many bunns as can be set into a dish without crowding. Make a custard of five eggs to a quart of milk, half a cup of sugar, a little salt and flavoring. Pour the custard over the bunns and let it stand till they are well soaked. If the custard is all absorbed, fill up the dish and bake three quarters of an hour.

CHOCOLATE CUSTARD.—Beat seven eggs separately; to the yolks add one fourth of a pound of white sugar; stir in the whites; dissolve one fourth of a pound of chocolate in one pint of hot milk, add one and a half pints of cream; give it one boil, turn it into the egg, stirring all the time. Strain it into a pitcher, set the pitcher into boiling water, stirring the custard constantly until it thickens. To be used in glasses to eat cold.

CUSTARD.—To one quart of milk take six eggs, one cup of sugar, a little salt and flavoring. Put the milk in the milk boiler and scald it; then pour it into the eggs and sugar, after they are well beaten; add a small piece of butter; put it into a pudding dish and bake fifteen or twenty minutes.

CHRISTMAS PUDDING. — One pound of bread crumbs or pounded crackers; wet them with milk, let it stand until well soaked but not too thin; add eight well beaten eggs, half a pound of sugar, the same of suet, a cup of molasses, a cup of brandy, a tablespoon of salt, one and a half pounds of stoned raisins, half a pound of citron cut fine, one pound of currants, (or chopped figs) one nutmeg, half a teaspoon of mace, one teaspoon of cloves, one grated lemon rind, and a teaspoon of soda. Boil in a mould, or floured pudding bag, five hours. To be served with rich brandy or wine sauce. It adds very much to the appearance to pour over it half a cup of brandy and set fire to it before sending it to the table.

EVE'S PUDDING.—Half a pound of bread crumbs, one pint of milk, four eggs, half a pound of suet, chopped fine, one fourth of a pound of chopped apples, the juice and grated rind of one lemon, and half a teaspoon of soda. Put into a mould and boil three hours.

FROZEN PUDDING. — Butter a pudding mould. Take stale fruit and sponge cake, put a layer of cake at the bottom of the mould, then a layer of jelly or jam, then a layer of cake, and so on till the mould is two thirds full. Turn on some good wine or brandy. Make a good boiled custard, and fill the mould with it; let it stand till the cake is soft. Let it stand covered in salt and ice seven or eight hours. When you wish to turn it out of the mould dip it for a second in hot water, and turn on to the dish.

ORANGE PUDDING. — Half a pound of bread crumbs soaked in half a pint of boiled milk; strain through a cullender; add one fourth of a pound of sugar, half a teaspoon of soda, half a pint of sweet orange juice, the grated rind of one orange and five eggs beaten separately; bake in a quick oven. —Wine sauce.

LEMON MERINGUE PUDDING.—One quart milk, two cups bread crumbs, four eggs, half cup butter, one cup white sugar, one large lemon, the juice and half the rind grated. Soak the bread in the milk, add the beaten yolk, with the butter and sugar rubbed to a cream, also the lemon. Bake in a buttered dish until firm and browned slightly; cover with a meringue made of the whites whipped to a stiff froth, with three tablespoons of powdered white sugar and a little lemon juice. Brown slightly.

CORN STARCH MERINGUE.—Four eggs, one quart milk, three fourths cup sugar, four teaspoons corn starch, half a cup of jelly or jam. Heat the milk to boiling, and stir in the corn starch which has been previously dissolved in cold milk; boil fifteen minutes, stirring all the time; remove from the fire, and, while hot, add gradually the yolks of the eggs, beaten up with the sugar; flavor with lemon or vanilla. Pour this into a pudding dish well buttered, and bake until the custard begins to set. Then put on the whites, beaten to a stiff froth, sweetened, and flavored. Brown slightly. Eat cold.

IRISH POTATO PUDDING.—Weigh one pound of potatoes after they are pared, boil them, and, when *well* done, pour off the water; let them dry. Mash them while they are still hot, add a pint of cream or rich milk, butter the size of an egg, a small cup of sugar, a gill of wine or the juice of one lemon, four eggs, beaten light, and a little salt. Bake in a deep dish, or use pie crust and make into pies.

SWEET POTATO PUDDING.—Five eggs, one fourth pound butter, one fourth pound sugar, as much mashed sweet potato, cold, as will thicken it; a glass of brandy, the juice and grated rind of a lemon, and spice, if you like. Bake in a deep buttered dish, or in pies.

STEAMED BATTER PUDDING.—One cup sugar, three eggs, one cup sweet milk, one heaping teaspoon baking powder, a little salt, flour enough to make the batter a little thicker than the batter for pancakes; steam twenty minutes. *Sauce for same.*—One cup sugar, mixed with one tablespoon of flour, and butter the size of an egg. Rub well together and pour on boiling water until as thick as cream. Flavor with vanilla.

A NICE PUDDING.—Six eggs, six tablespoons of flour, half a pint of sweet milk and a pinch of salt. Beat the eggs well, stir in the flour, add salt and milk; flour your sack, have the water boiling, put the mixture into the sack, tie loosely to allow for rising. Boil three quarters of an hour. *Sauce.*—Three large tablespoons of butter, same amount of white sugar, and water; grate in a little nutmeg. If for plum pudding add a glass of old port wine.

BAKE DAY PUDDING.—Take two cups light dough, roll it thin, spread on a layer of jam or any fruit you may like, or you can work all through it half a pound of raisins. Let the dough thus prepared rise until light. Steam an hour, sometimes longer. Eaten with sugar and cream.

FARMER'S PUDDING.—One quart sweet milk, three eggs, flour enough to make a thick batter, just so that it will pour, and one and a half teaspoons baking powder. Pare and quarter enough apples to fill a gallon pan; pour the batter over the apples and bake. Serve with sugar and cream.

PUFF PUDDING.—Four eggs well beaten, three cups sweet milk, two cups flour, one third cup butter. Beat until all is in a foam. Have ready some nicely buttered cups, fill half full, and bake in a quick oven until nicely browned. Eat with cream or sauce.

APPLE DUMPLING, BOILED.—One pound of flour, half a pound of suet. Chop the suet in a little of the flour, to prevent its caking—chop as fine as meal; add a teaspoon of salt and two teaspoons of baking powder. Mix with enough water or milk for a paste. Roll it, but not as thin as for pie crust. Pare, core and quarter a dozen large apples. Put the four quarters together, cut the paste into squares, to cover the apples. Tie in a cloth, well floured, and boil till done.

APPLE DUMPLINGS, BAKED. Roll out some dough thicker than pie crust, and enclose a handful of ripe apples, sliced—covered with butter and sugar, and a few bits of cinnamon bark. Bring the edges together, as in any other dumpling. When as many are made as desired, place them side by side in a pudding pan, spread butter and sugar over them—pour in enough water to fill the pan. Place in the oven and bake a nice brown. Cook moderately.

FANCY DESSERTS.

APPLE CHARLOTTE.—Beat two cups of nice apple sauce, well sweetened and flavored, to a high froth, with the whipped whites of three eggs; make it into a mound in a glass dish and cover it with lady's fingers or other small sponge cakes fitted neatly together. Send around cream with it.

APPLE SNOW.—Peel and core five large apples, boil them in a little water until soft enough to pass through a sieve; sweeten and beat with them the beaten whites of three eggs. Serve with cream.

CHARLOTTE RUSSE.—One pint of rich cream, sweetened; add wine to taste, whip very light; steep one ounce of gelatine in half a pint of water until reduced one half. Line a dish with sponge cake and pour on the cream. Set on ice to congeal.

MRS. W. S. H——.

ICE CREAM.—To one gallon of milk take eight eggs and one and a half pounds of white sugar. Cook the eggs in half the milk; add the sugar while warm: when cold add the rest of the milk, and flavor to taste. Freeze.

MRS. S. S. L——.

ICE CREAM, No. 2. — Two pounds of sugar to one gallon of cream. Whip the cream and flavor to taste. When half frozen add the beaten whites of six eggs.

TAPIOCA CREAM.—Two tablespoonfuls of tapioca, which has been previously soaked in cold water several hours, one quart of milk, and a little salt. When the tapioca has boiled soft, remove it from the fire. Stir in one whole egg, the yolks of three, a cup of sugar, and flavoring to suit the taste. Put on to boil ten or fifteen minutes, stirring constantly. Beat the whites and stir them in just before taking from the fire. Pour into a dish and serve hot or cold. Two eggs with one tablespoon of corn starch will answer.

MRS. W. W. B——.

ORANGE CREAM.—Make a rich pie crust and bake it in a pan; quarter some oranges and lay them on the crust. Take the yolks of four eggs, a little wine and sugar, according to taste, also a little orange juice. Stir it on the fire until thick. Beat the whites to a stiff froth; stir all together and pour over the fruit.

WHIPPED CREAM.—Dissolve half a box of Coxe's gelatine in a little hot water, and set it aside to cool. Sweeten a half gallon of thick, sweet, rich cream, using pulverized sugar; flavor with vanilla; add the gelatine, and whip with an egg-beater until very stiff. Serve in float glasses.

MISS ANNA C——.

Hen's Nest.—Get nice eggs, make a hole at one end and empty the shells; fill them with blanc mange. When it is cold and hard take off the shells. Pare the yellow rind from six lemons and boil them in water until tender; then cut them into thin strips to resemble straw, and preserve them in sugar;. fill a small, deep dish half full of nice jelly, and when it is set, put on the strips of lemon in the form of a nest, and lay the eggs in it.

PIES.

PASTRY for Pies.—Take half as much lard as flour, add a little salt and a cup of very cold water. Mix all together, but mix the lard very thoroughly in the flour before pouring in the water.

MRS. WM. H——.

PUFF PASTE.—To every pound of flour take three fourths of a pound of butter, the yolk of an egg, and ice cold water. Chop half the butter in the flour, then add the beaten yolk and as much water as needed. Work all into a dough, roll out thin, and spread on some of the butter; fold closely, buttered side in, and re-roll; repeat until the butter is all used up. Keep in a cool place until you wish to use it.

MINCE MEAT.—Three pounds of lean meat, (beef) boiled; when cold chop fine; one pound beef suet, chopped fine, five pounds of apples after they are pared, cored and chopped, one pound Sultana raisins picked and washed, two pounds raisins seeded and chopped, three fourths pound citron cut fine, two tablespoons each of cinnamon and mace, one nutmeg grated, one tablespoon each of ground allspice, cloves and salt, two and a half pounds of brown sugar, one quart sweet cider, sherry wine, or the vinegar left from sweet pickles, and one pint brandy. Keep in stone jars well covered. It is an improvement to put in two chopped lemons.

CREAM PIE.—One pint sweet milk, one tablespoon corn-starch, previously dissolved in cold milk, half a cup of sugar, one egg, beaten and put in with the corn starch, and a piece of butter; Flavor. Boil until thick. *Cake.* Three eggs beaten separately, three tablespoons water, one cup sugar, one and a half cups flour, two teaspoons baking powder; add the whites of eggs last; bake quickly in two pie pans; split open and spread custard between; sprinkle the top with sugar; eat cold.

CREAM PIE, No. 2.—Beat the yolks of three eggs very light, with a cup of sugar; add the grated rind of a lemon, a pinch of salt, and half a cup of corn-starch dissolved in a little cold milk. Pour on to this a pint of boiling milk, stirring all the time. Return to the fire until it thickens, *stirring all the* time. Line a pie pan with some good pie crust and bake it. Fill the shell with the custard, and cover the top with a meringue made of the whites of three eggs, three ounces of powdered sugar, and the juice of the lemon. Return to the oven and brown slightly. Vanilla can be used instead of lemon, if preferred.

LEMON PIE.—The juice of one lemon, one teacup of white sugar, one teacup of water, one egg, and one teaspoon of flour; two crusts. This makes one pie.

LEMON PIE, No 2.—One tablespoon of butter, three fourths of a cup of sugar, three eggs, and the juice of one lemon. Bake in open shells of paste. Cream the sugar and butter, stir the lemon into the beaten yolks and bake. Beat the whites to a stiff meringue with three tablespoons of powdered sugar, and a little rose water. When the pies are done, take them from the oven, spread the meringue over the top, return them to the oven, and brown slightly.
MRS. JOS. P——.

LEMON PIE, No. 3. One cup of sugar, one tablespoon of corn starch, a piece of butter the size of an egg, one lemon, one teacup of boiling water, and one egg. Mix the corn starch with a little cold water, and stir it into the boiling water. Let it boil up, then pour it on to the butter and sugar; when cold beat in the egg and the juice and grated rind of the lemon.
MRS. C. V. J——.

LEMON PIE, No. 4.—The juice and grated rind of one large lemon, one cup of sugar, the yolks of two eggs, three tablespoons of flour, and one and a half cups of milk. Beat the whites with four tablespoons of sugar, and put over the pie when nearly done. Brown slightly in the oven.
MRS. J. H. M——.

LEMON PIE, No. 5.—One pint of boiling water, a piece of butter, the grated rind and juice of one lemon, one cup of sugar; when the water is boiling pour in two beaten yolks, with one and a half tablespoons of corn starch mixed with a little cold water; stir constantly until it thickens, and then pour into open shells previously baked. When nearly done, spread the whites beaten with two tablespoons of powdered sugar, over the top. Return to the oven, and brown slightly.

MRS. EVA S———.

LEMON CUSTARD PIE.—Three eggs, one and a half pints of milk one teacup of sugar, three tablespoons of flour, and one tablespoon of lemon extract. Boil the milk; mix flour, sugar and yolks with a little milk. Pour into the boiling milk. Then fill the pies, and bake. Beat the whites with half a teacup of sugar and a little lemon. Spread over the pie and bake to a delicate brown.

MRS. S. S. L———.

PUMPKIN PIE.—One quart of strained pumpkin, two quarts of milk, one pint of cream, one teaspoon of salt, four teaspoons of ginger, two teaspoons of cinnamon, and six eggs.

MRS. S. S. L———.

CUSTARD PIE. Take two eggs, two tablespoons of sugar, one tablespoon of flour, and one pint of sweet milk. Flavor with nutmeg. For one pie.

MRS. S. S. L———.

Apple Custard Pie.—Stew some apples so soft that they will run through a sieve. To a quart of stewed apples add two teacups of sugar, one pint of milk, half a cup of butter, five eggs, a grated lemon peel, and bake in puff paste.

Pine-Apple Pie. — A grated pine-apple, its weight in sugar, half its weight in butter, one cupful of cream, and five eggs beaten separately. Cream the butter, sugar and yolks until very light, then add the cream, pine-apple and whites. Bake with one crust. Eat cold.

Apple Meringue Pie.—Stew, and sweeten juicy apples, when you have pared and sliced them; mash smooth and season with nutmeg. Fill your crusts and bake till done. Spread over the apples a thick meringue, made by beating the whites to a stiff froth, sweetened with a tablespoon of powdered sugar to each egg. Flavor with rose or vanilla. Brown slightly in the oven. Peaches are even more delicious when used in the same manner.

Green Apple Pie.—Pare, quarter, core and stew, nice tart apples in enough water to prevent them from burning; when tender, sweeten very sweet with white sugar; fill the crust, grate on a little nutmeg, cover, and bake until quite done.

Raisin Pie.—One pound of raisins; pour over them one quart of boiling water and keep adding so that there will be one quart when done. Grate the rind of one lemon into a cup of sugar, then add three teaspoons of flour and one egg; mix well together. Turn the raisins over the mixture stirring the while. Bake as other pies.

GREEN TOMATO PIE.—Select nice, smooth tomatoes, pare them very thin, slice them into a pie-dish lined with puff paste. Put half a cup of sugar and a few bits of butter to a pie and sift on a little flour. Use sliced lemon, lemon extract or nutmeg for flavoring. Put on the upper crust carefully, so that the juice will not escape in baking.

RIPE TOMATO PIE.—Prepare the pastry as for an apple pie; slice in as many ripe tomatoes as will fill the plate; sprinkle a single handful of flour over; it add two teaspoons of lemon extract and one teacup of white sugar. Wet the edge of the bottom crust before covering with the top. The fruit will be cooked as soon as the crusts are.

APPLE CUSTARD PIE, No. 2.—Peel tart apples and stew them until soft, not leaving much water in them. Strain through a cullender; beat three eggs for each pie to be baked, and put in one third of a cup each of butter and sugar for each pie; season with nutmeg, cover with frosting as in lemon pie, and return for a few minutes to the oven.

COCOANUT PIE.—One quart new milk, the yolks of five eggs, one cup sugar, the grated rind and juice of one lemon, and one good sized cocoanut; whip the whites well, add sugar to taste, and put on top of the pie when baked. Brown again slightly.

MRS. G. S. B——.

VEGETABLES.

VEGETABLES should be carefully cleansed from insects, and nicely washed. Every kind of vegetable, except green peas, should lie in cold water some time before cooking. Boil them in plenty of water and *drain* them the *moment they are done* enough. In order to boil vegetables of a good green color take care that the water boils when they are put in. Make them boil fast. Do not cover them, but watch them. Take them out immediately after they are done, else the color will change.

BAKED POTATOES.—Wash and wipe them dry, put them into the oven with the skins on, and bake three fourths to one hour. When half done prick them with a fork, to let out the steam and prevent them from being soggy.

WHIPPED POTATOES.— Whip boiled potatoes to creamy lightness, with a fork; beat in butter, milk, pepper and salt, and, at last, the frothed white of an egg. Toss irregularly upon a dish and set them in the oven two minutes to reheat, but do not color.

MASHED POTATOES, BROWNED. — Whip boiled potatoes light with cream, butter and salt; pile on a greased pie dish, and brown in a good oven.

VEGETABLES.

Pone-De-Tat.—One dozen medium sized potatoes boiled, peeled and sliced; put a layer of potatoes, and finely crumbed cheese, with butter, pepper, salt and ground mustard between the layers. Have the last layer of cheese. Put into a quick oven and bake twenty minutes.

MRS. K. R——.

Scalloped Potatoes.—Slice cold boiled potatoes very thin and small; put one quart of them into a baking dish, in layers, with two even teaspoons of salt, two thirds of a teaspoon of pepper, and two and a half ounces of butter; pour half a pint of cream or milk over the whole; cover the potatoes with grated bread, a little pepper salt and small bits of butter. Bake until thoroughly heated and browned.

Sweet Potatoes.—Boil softly, peel carefully and lay in a greased dripping pan, in a good oven. As they begin to crust over baste them frequently with a little butter and water. A little sugar sprinkled over them is an addition. When brown they are done.

Stuffed Cabbage.—One common sized head of cabbage, scooped out, with the cap left to put on, one teacup of chopped ham and the cabbage that came out, one teacup of bread or crackers rolled fine, butter, pepper, salt and mustard to taste; boil or steam until done and serve with drawn butter.

MRS. K. R——.

COLD SLAW.—Cut cabbage fine, sprinkle over it pepper and salt and set it in a cool place. Take two eggs, or the yolks of three, five tablespoons of vinegar, three teaspoons of sugar, half a teaspoon of made mustard and one teaspoon of butter; put them in a tin cup and stir them over the fire, until it becomes a smooth paste; let it become cold and then mix with the cabbage ready for use.

SLAW, No. 2.—Cut cabbage fine and sprinkle salt over it; then take the hands and squeeze the cabbage thoroughly, until it is well seasoned: sprinkle over some sugar and squeeze again, the same as with the salt; next, pepper to taste and pour vinegar over it, and it is ready for use.

MRS. W. W. B———.

CELERY SLAW.—Cabbage, celery, and two hard boiled eggs, chopped fine: season to taste with salt, pepper and mustard; moisten with vinegar.

TOMATOES, STEWED.—Scald and skin the desired number, and place in a stew pan without water; let them simmer for half an hour. Add butter, pepper, salt, a spoonful of white sugar, and a little cream. Grate a few bits of stale bread over all. Boil up once, and serve hot.

SCALLOPED TOMATOES.—Put a layer of bread crumbs on the bottom of a buttered pudding dish, and on them a layer of tomatoes; sprinkle with salt, pepper and a few bits of butter, (if liked a few bits of onion,) another layer of bread crumbs, another of tomatoes, and seasoning. Then a top layer of bread crumbs. Bake, covered, until boiling hot, and brown quickly.

STUFFED TOMATOES.—Get them as large and firm as possible; cut a round place in the top of each, and scrape out all the soft parts, and mix them with stale bread crumbs, corn, onions, parsley, butter, pepper and salt; chop very fine, and fill the tomatoes carefully; Bake in a moderately hot oven, put a little butter in the pan, and see that they do not burn nor become dry.

BAKED TOMATOES.—Pour boiling water over them to remove the skins. Put them into a deep, well buttered dish, sprinkle salt, pepper, butter and powdered crackers over them. Bake three fourths of an hour. Baste occasionally with the liquor that comes from them.

GREEN CORN PUDDING.—One quart of milk, three beaten eggs, one dozen ears of grated corn, one tablespoon each of butter, sugar and salt. Bake in a covered pudding dish one hour.

CORN OYSTERS.—Grate enough of green corn to make a pint of pulp; add one teacup of flour, one half teacup of butter, one or two eggs, salt and pepper to suit taste. Drop with a spoon, and fry in hot butter or lard.

MRS. J. C. J——.

SUCCOTASH—Cut off all the corn from the cobs, and, an hour before wanted, put the cobs and a few shelled beans into water to boil; let the cobs boil one hour; take them out and put in the corn, and boil it half an hour. Have as little water as possible; when done add butter, pepper and salt. Pork boiled with the corn and beans gives a good flavor.

CANNED CORN.—One quart of corn, one quart of water, one small teaspoon of tartaric acid; boil half an hour; when you open the can, pour off the sour water, and pour on boiling water; put in a little soda to sweeten the corn, but not enough to yellow it; if so, pour back some of the sour water, season with salt, pepper, butter and cream.

MRS. S. S. L——.

CANNED CORN.—Three pints of water to half a gallon of cut corn and two teaspoons of tartaric acid; when opened for use add half a teaspoon of soda.

MRS. I. N. S——.

STEWED MUSHROOMS.—Be sure the mushrooms are fresh; cut off the part of the stalk which grew in the earth; wash them, put them into a sauce pan with half a pint of water, one ounce of butter, the juice of one lemon, pepper and salt. Boil ten minutes, stirring all the time; thicken half a cup of cream with some flour, stir it in, and let it boil once. Send to the table in a covered dish.

MACCARONI.—Break the maccaroni into pieces two inches long; put it to soak in cold water one hour; let it boil slowly for half an hour, add a little salt and a cup of milk, and let it boil till tender; add a small piece of butter and serve as a plain vegetable.

BAKED MACCARONI.—After soaking as above, let it boil in milk half an hour; have ready some finely grated cheese; butter a small dish, and lay in the maccaroni with a little salt sprinkled over it. Put the grated cheese on top, and put it into the oven to brown.

OYSTER MACCARONI.—Boil maccaroni in a cloth to keep it straight; put a layer in a dish seasoned with butter, pepper and salt, then a layer of oysters, and so alternating until the dish is full. Mix some grated bread with beaten egg, spread it over the top, and bake.

CAULIFLOWER.—Tie in a net and cook about forty-five minutes, in boiling salt water. Drain, lay in a deep dish, blossom upward, and pour over it half a cup of rich drawn butter with the juice of a lemon stirred in.

BAKED BEANS.—Take one quart of white beans, pick them and soak them over night in plenty of water. In the morning pour off the water, put the beans in the pot and fill with cold water; take three quarters of a pound of salt pork, scrape the rind and score it, put it into the pot before all the beans are in, letting the rind of the pork come even with the top of the beans; when tender, put them in a deep dish or pan, pork on top, and bake a light brown.

BEETS.—Wash, cut off the tops, boil until quite tender; scrape, cut into round slices and put in a dish, pour over them one tablespoon of butter heated with as much vinegar, and season with pepper and salt.

STEWED CELERY.—Scrape and cut into short bits, cook tender in hot salted water; pour this off, add enough cold milk to cover the celery, heat to a boil, stir in a good spoonful of butter rolled in flour, pepper and salt. Stew five minutes longer.

A little sugar added to parsnips and turnips, while boiling, is a great improvement.

CANDY.

THREE large cups sugar, a half cup of vinegar, a half cup of water. Mix together and boil, without stirring, until done. When done add a teaspoon of butter and a pinch of soda.

PEPPERMINT DROPS.—One pound powdered sugar, sifted, and the whites of three or four eggs; add ten or twelve drops of oil of peppermint, beat well and drop on writing paper.

COCOANUT DROPS.—The whites of three eggs, six tablespoons of flour, one cup of sugar and two cups of grated cocoanut.

CREAM CANDY.—Three pounds loaf sugar, half pint of water; cook on a slow fire half an hour; add one teaspoon of gum arabic dissolved and one tablespoon vinegar; boil until brittle and pull into long sticks.

BLACK CROOK CANDY.—One pint of molasses, half a pint of brown sugar and one pound of prepared cocoanut. Boil till it candies.

COCOANUT CANDY.—Boil half a pound of loaf sugar with two tablespoons of water; then stir in half a pound of grated cocoanut, flavor with lemons, and pour into buttered tins.

Sugar Candy.—Two pounds of coffee sugar, one pint of water, half a cup of vinegar and a piece of butter the size of an egg. Flavor to taste and pull same as molasses candy.

Chocolate Caramel.—Two cups brown sugar, one cup molasses, half cup of milk, butter the size of an egg, half package of Baker's chocolate, grated and dissolved in the milk and one teaspoon of vanilla: boil; when hard turn out one fourth inch thick on buttered tins; when partly cool mark it off in squares with a knife.

Molasses Candy.—One cup of sugar, one cup of molasses, three quarters of a cup of water, butter the size of a hickory nut.

Cream Candy, No. 2.—Two pounds of light sugar, one teacup of water, two tablespoons of butter, one tablespoon of vinegar; flavor to taste.

Butter Scotch.—One pint of syrup, one teacup of brown sugar, one tablespoon of butter, one tablespoon of vinegar.

Splendid Candy.—Three teacups of white sugar, one and a half cups of sweet milk, to dissolve it; boil till done, and flavor with vanilla; stir until hard.

Horehound Candy.—Prepare a strong decoction by boiling two ounces of the dried herb in one and a half pints of water for half an hour; strain this, and add three and a half pounds of brown sugar; boil over a hot fire until it reaches the requisite degree of hardness, when it may be poured out into flat tin trays, previously well greased, and marked into sticks or squares with a knife, as it becomes cool enough to retain its shape.

LEMON AND PEPPERMINT DROPS.—Take two ounces of water to one pound of sugar; set it over the fire and allow it to nearly boil, keeping it continually stirred. It must not actually come to a full boil, but must be removed from the fire just as soon as the bubbles denote that the boiling point is reached. Allow the syrup to cool a little, stirring all the time; add strong essence of lemon or peppermint to suit the taste, and drop it on sheets of white paper. They should be kept in a warm place a few hours to dry. In the season of fruits delicious drops may be made by substituting the juice of fresh fruits, as strawberry, raspberry, lemon, pineapple or banana.

TAFFY.—Three pounds of the best brown sugar, boiled with one and a half pints of water until the candy hardens in cold water; add half a pound of fresh butter which will soften the candy; boil a few minutes until it again hardens, and pour it into trays. Flavor with lemon, if desired.

POP CORN BALLS.—Take three quarts of popped corn; boil half a pint of molasses about fifteen minutes, then put the corn into a large pan and pour the molasses over it, stirring briskly until thoroughly mixed. Then, with the hands, make into balls of the desired size.

MISCELLANEOUS KNOWLEDGE.

CEMENT.—Mix together equal parts of litharge and glycerine to the consistency of thick cream. This is useful for mending stone jars, or any earthen ware, stopping leaks in tin pans, wash boilers, or iron teakettles; also in fastening lamp tops. The articles should not be used until the cement hardens, which will take from one day to a week.

FURNITURE POLISH.—Mix equal parts of boiled linseed oil and kerosene. Apply it with a flannel rag, and rub the article well with dry flannel.

WASHING FLUID.—One box of refined potash, five cents worth of ammonia and five cents worth of salts of tartar. Put the potash in a jar and pour over it a gallon of boiling water. When cool add salts of tartar and ammonia; cover tightly; soak the clothes in cold water over night. In the morning cut half a bar of soap into the boiler, and when it is dissolved add one teacup of the fluid. Wring out the clothes, put them into the boiler and let them boil a few minutes. After this they will need little rubbing, and very little soap.

To Clean Ostrich Plumes.—White ones can be cleaned by taking four ounces of white soap, cutting it into small pieces, dissolving it in four pints of water, rather hot, and making a lather, and then dipping the feathers in the mixture and washing them gently with the hands for about ten minutes. Rinse them in hot water, and shake them till dry. Ostrich tips can be curled by holding them in the steam from water until they are damp, then drawing each fibre separately over the blade of a blunt knife.

Silver Polish.—Mix half an ounce of prepared chalk, two ounces of alcohol, and two ounces of aqua ammonia. Apply the mixture with a piece of cotton flannel, and rub the article to be polished with chamois skin.

Pansies are nice for winter decorations if pressed between layers of cotton. When mixed with ferns they are nice to put in white willow baskets.

To Cleanse a Meerschaum Pipe.—Use strong coffee. Let it stand in the bowl a short time, or draw it back and forth through the stem.

Wash chamois skin in cold water with plenty of soap. Rinse it in cold water.

If fresh unslacked lime, in small quantities, say a quart, be kept in refrigerators it will gradually absorb all the moisture in the provision chamber. A little experience will soon enable persons to know when to remove the lime.

Ants can be gotten rid of by washing the shelves clean, and, while they are damp, rubbing on them fine salt, pulverized camphor, five cents worth of calomel, cayenne pepper, or powdered cloves.

To destroy house flies.—Take one half teaspoon black pepper, one teaspoon brown sugar and one teaspoon cream. Mix them well together in a saucer, and place the mixture where the flies are likely to be.

To clean marble.—Apply benzine liberally, and rub it off with a clean flannel. Never apply soap to marble, as it takes off the polish. Grease spots may be removed, by the application of powdered magnesia.

To keep a stove from rusting in summer.—Rub kerosene on it in the spring.

Mirrors should never be hung where the sun shines directly upon them.

To remove Fruit or Wine Stains wet the spots with hartshorn.

To brighten a zinc bath tub.—Throw in a handful of salt, wet with vinegar, and rub the tub with a flannel cloth.

Washing.—Have plenty of boiling water, and to each boiler-full add two or three tablespoons of pulverized borax. Use some of this water for every tubful of clothes; use soap on the most soiled clothes and rub them on the board. Do not boil the clothes. Have a tub nearly full of boiling borax water, into which put the clothes that have been rubbed. Let them remain an hour, or until you are ready to rinse them. Rinse in clear water *without* borax. Use very little bluing. Add a teaspoon of borax to each quart of starch, and it will keep the starch from sticking, and add to the lustre.

SOAP.—One ounce of pulverized borax, one pound of the best brown soap cut in small pieces, three quarts of water; put all in a kettle, and keep it on the back part of the stove until the soap is dissolved, stirring frequently; it must not come to a boil. Use it with a piece of old soft flannel. It cleanses paint without injury, is better for washing clothes than any other, and is beneficial to the hands.

FOR CHILLS AND FEVER.—Eat nine grains of black pepper *after* each meal. Try it.

IN CANNING FRUIT wring a towel or cloth out in hot water and wrap it around the jar, having several thicknesses at the bottom; set the jar in a pan and fill it with hot fruit or liquid, without fear.

Sulphuric acid rubbed on the edges of drawers in a bureau or wash-stand will prevent their swelling in damp weather.

Keep fresh lard in tin vessels.

RENOVATING MIXTURE for removing grease and killing bed bugs. One quart of soft rain water, two ounces aqua ammonia, one teaspoon saltpetre, one ounce soap (Babbit's) finely scraped. Mix all and let it stand a few hours. Apply with a small brush to every place the bugs infest. It is certain death. *To remove grease.* Cover the grease spots with the mixture, rub well with a brush or sponge, then wash off with clear water. It will not injure any more than water. It is nice for cleaning carpets.

To BEAT THE WHITES of eggs quickly add a pinch of salt. The cooler the eggs the better.

In boiling eggs always put them into boiling water. It prevents the yolk from coloring black.

Never wash raisins to be used in sweet dishes; it will make the pudding heavy; wipe them with a dry towel.

To brown sugar for sauce or puddings put it in a perfectly dry sauce pan. If the pan is the least bit wet the sugar will burn.

Water used in mixing bread must be tepid; if too hot the loaf will be full of holes.

Frozen plants may be restored by sprinkling them with cold water, and setting them in the dark for twenty four hours, in a temperature of not more than fifty degrees.

A cloth dampened with wine and put over cakes will keep them fresh for a long time.

CURE FOR HAY FEVER.—A tablespoonful of pepper vinegar taken at night, or when the chilly sensation is felt.

To REMOVE MOTH PATCHES.—Put a tablespoonful of flour of sulphur, or, better still, lac of sulphur, into a pint bottle of rum. Apply to the moth patches once a day and they will disappear in two or three weeks.

Remedy for Burns.—One ounce of pulverized borax, one quart of boiling water, and half an ounce of pulverized alum. Shake up well and bottle. Wrap the burn in soft linen and keep it constantly wet with the solution. Do not remove the linen until the burn is cured.

Cure for Cholera.—Take equal parts of tincture of cayenne pepper, tincture of opium, tincture of rhubarb, essence of peppermint and spirits of camphor, and mix them well. Dose, fifteen to thirty drops, in a little cold water, according to the age of the patient and the violence of the symptoms repeated every fifteen minutes until relief is obtained.

Hair should be well washed, every five or six weeks, in warm water and one or two tablespoons of ammonia. Dry it thoroughly before tying— Brush one hundred strokes every morning with a stiff brush, and clip the ends once every month, and you will soon be well paid for your trouble.

Cut Flowers should first be dipped in hot water, to wilt them, and *then* placed in cool water to revive them—they do not wilt so soon the second time.

Pearls are kept brilliant by keeping them in common dry magnesia, instead of cotton wool used in jewel caskets.

Burns.—Equal parts of sweet oil and coal oil will be found excellent for burns.

CHILBLAINS OR FROZEN FEET. — Take fresh or rancid lard, burn it till it waxes; then pour it over frozen snow or ice. Rub the frozen feet with it, and hold them to the fire. This is well worth trying.

SLEEPLESSNESS can be relieved by laying a wet cloth on the back of the neck, with a dry cloth outside.

WHOOPING COUGH REMEDY. — Mix one sliced lemon, half a pint of flax seed, two ounces of honey one quart of water, and simmer, *not boil*, four hours. Dose, one tablespoonful four times a day, and one after each fit of coughing.

BUNIONS. — Use pulverized saltpetre and sweet oil. Put five cents worth of saltpetre into enough sweet oil to dissolve it. Shake well and rub the inflamed joints, night and morning.

SMALL POX CURE. — One ounce of cream of tartar, dissolved in a pint of boiling water, and drank when cold, at short intervals, is a preventive as well as a curative—and is excellent for a rough, pimply face.

DIPHTHERIA. — A teaspoonful of powder of sulphur, in a wineglass of water. Stir with the *finger*, not with a spoon. Mix well, and use as a gargle, and occasionally swallow it.

THE SICK ROOM.

EVERY family should keep a small quantity of chlorate of potash. There is nothing equal to it for a simple ulcerated sore throat. Dissolve one teaspoonful in a tumbler of water, and occasionally take a teaspoonful of the solution, so as to gargle the throat. Nothing is better than this for chapped hands or a pimply face. Wash them in a weak solution.

BEEF BROTH WITH TAPIOCA.—Cut a pound of lean, juicy beef into pieces, and soak for an hour in a quart of cold water; then put it to cook in the same water, and cover closely to keep in the steam. Simmer for two hours and strain; if there was the least fat on the meat cool the broth and remove it from the surface. Soak a quarter of a cup of tapioca in a little cold water and boil it half an hour in the broth; season with salt, pepper and a few drops of lemon juice. Serve with rice, thin crackers or dry toast.

CHICKEN JELLY.—Pound half a chicken, bones and meat, until all are well softened, then cover with cold water and cook slowly, until the meat is tasteless and about two cups of the liquid is left in the pan. Strain and season the liquor and turn it into small, wet moulds; keep in a cool place, and, when *wanted*, turn out a form on a dish: garnish with sprigs of parsley; serve cold with thin slices of bread and butter.

CREAMED CRACKERS.—Split six Boston crackers; place them in a plate and pour boiling water over them. As soon as they are slightly softened pour off the water, sprinkle slightly with salt, and pour some sweet cream over them.

FRUIT BLANC MANGE.—The juice of any fruit may be used; if not sweet enough add sugar. Mix a tablespoonful of corn starch with a little cold water, and stir into it half a pint of boiling fruit juice; cook until it thickens and then pour it into a wet mould. Serve cold with sweetened cream, to which add a little flavoring.

TAPIOCA JELLY.—Soak half a cup of tapioca in a pint of water for four hours, then cook it in a double boiler until the tapioca is soft and clear looking. Season with only a little sugar, and lemon juice, and pour it into small, wet moulds. Serve with sweet cream.

ICELAND MOSS BLANC MANGE.—Wash the moss thoroughly in several waters, and soak it an hour. To a handful allow a quart of rich, sweet milk; put the moss in when the milk is boiling hot, and let it simmer until the moss is soft. Then strain, sweeten, and flavor with lemon juice, and put it into wet moulds. Serve cold with cream and sugar. Iceland moss cooked in water instead of milk, and made thin enough to be taken as a drink, is soothing and nourishing, and excellent for colds and sore throats.

Pearl Barley.—Wash the barley in several waters and tie it in a cloth loosely, so that it will have room to swell; boil it four hours in water enough to cover it, adding more as it becomes necessary. Serve with sweet milk.

Barley Water is made by boiling an ounce of barley in a quart of water until it is reduced one half, when it must be strained, cooled, salted, and sweetened, as the patient may desire. It is a refreshing and soothing drink for persons suffering with inflammation of the mucous membrane.

SUPPLEMENT.

SPONGE FOR WINTER USE.—Boil four good sized potatoes, until thoroughly done, in plenty of water; then take them off the stove, pour off the water, and, with a spoon, mash and beat the potatoes until they are foamy; when *warm*, not hot, put in a tablespoonful of salt, a pint of flour, and the potato water, which was previously poured off. Mix to a tolerably stiff batter; then pour in a teacup of *warm* water *in which* a cake or half a cake of compressed yeast has been dissolved. Set it away to rise. This will keep a week.

GOOD YEAST BREAD.—Measure four quarts of sifted flour; take out a pint of it, and place the remainder in the bread bowl. Mix through it, a tablespoonful of lard, and a very little salt, and pour in two pints (or two coffee cups) of *sponge for winter use*. Pour in enough luke-warm milk to make it of the right consistency; knead it thoroughly, and set it to rise; in two hours knead again. Make into loaves—about five; grease the *loaves* well—*not* the pan. Set to rise in the baking pan; when double the original size, they are ready for baking.

When *winter sponge* is not convenient it is best to dissolve half a cake of compressed yeast in a pint of *warm* water, and stir into it enough flour to make a tolerably thick batter, set it to rise, and in an hour or two, it is ready to pour into the flour for bread.

LONG BREAKFAST ROLLS.—Nearly two cups of sweet milk, half a cup of lard and butter mixed, half a cup of potato yeast, and flour enough to make it into dough. Let it rise over night. In the morning, add one beaten egg. Knead thoroughly again. With the hands make it into balls as large as a guinea egg, then roll it between the hands to make long rolls — three inches—place them close together, in even rows, in the pans. Let them rise until light. Bake.

APPLE FRITTERS.—Make a batter of one cup of sweet milk, two cups of flour, one heaping teaspoonful of baking powder, two eggs, and one tablespoon of sugar, with salt to taste. Heat the milk a *little*, add slowly the beaten yolks and sugar, *then* add the flour, and the *whites*. Stir all together, and throw in thin slices of nice tart apples, dipping the batter over them. Drop into boiling lard, in spoonfuls, with a piece of apple in each, and fry to a light brown.

BUCKWHEAT CAKES. Put one pint of warm sweet milk, and one pint of water into a stone crock; into which stir five cups of buckwheat flour; beat well until smooth, and, lastly, add one cup of yeast. Some persons prefer one tablespoon of sugar or molasses added. Set it to rise over night, and, if it is a little sour in the morning, add a pinch of soda.

PIE CRUST.—For one pie, take a double handful of flour, one fourth of a spoonful of salt, two *heaping* tablespoonfuls of lard, and as *little* water as will mix. Mix the lard *thoroughly* in the flour, before adding the cold water.

MRS. W. L. S.——

PRAIRIE CHICKEN.—Dress nicely, and wash thoroughly, in water with a little soda in it. Fill it with dressing, and tie down the legs and wings; place it in a steamer over hot water till it is done. Remove it to a dripping pan, cover it with butter, and sprinkle it with salt, pepper and flour; place it in the oven, baste it with the melted butter, and bake it a light brown.

QUAILS are nice, if stuffed with dressing, seasoned with salt, pepper and butter, put in a dripping pan, placed in the oven, and baked a nice brown. They must be basted frequently.

STEAMED CHICKENS.—After they have been carefully dressed, cut them up as for frying; place them in an iron pot (which must be set on *top* of the stove, not next to the blaze) with a little salt, pepper and ground ginger to taste, and a coffee cup of water to each chicken. Let it steam until thoroughly done, and, if the chicken is not very fat, add a little butter. Take up the chicken, and thicken the gravy with a little flour and cream.

Mock Duck.—Take a large round steak, pound it well, season it with salt and pepper, spread it with a thick layer of dressing as for turkey, and then roll it up; tie it with a cord, and place it in the dripping pan, with a little water. Season again as a roast, place it in the oven and bake, basting frequently. Remove the cord before sending it to the table.

Beefsteak cut into small squares, rolled in beaten egg, and bread crumbs, and then fried in hot lard, will be a palatable change.

Baked Ham.—Select a very small ham, wash it off nicely, and sprinkle it with pepper. Place it in a dripping pan in the oven, with a *little* water, and bake until done. It will take several hours;—Or first boil it, and then place it in the oven long enough to brown the outside nicely.

A well tried recipe for curing feet, pork, mutton, tongues and hams.—To one gallon of water take one and a half pounds of salt, half a pound of sugar, half an ounce of saltpetre, half an ounce of potash; use only a pure article of potash; if this cannot be obtained omit it altogether. Let these be boiled all together, until all the dirt from the sugar rises to the top, and is skimmed off. Then put it into a tub to cool, and, when cold, pour it over your beef or pork. The meat should be *well* covered with the pickle, and should not be put down, for at least two days after killing, during which time, it should be slightly sprinkled with powdered saltpetre. Meat pickled in this manner is unsurpassed for sweetness, delicacy and freshness of color.

SWEET PICKLE BEETS.—Boil them in a porcelain kettle until thoroughly done. When cool, cut them in slices as for the table; pour over them enough hot *spiced* vinegar to cover them. These are very nice and can be made in winter as wanted.

PICKLED ONIONS.—Take the small, silver skinned, white onions. Peel off the outer skin. Make a brine strong enough to float an egg, skim it well, and when it begins to cool pour it upon the onions. Let them stand in it (closely covered) until quite cold; then take them out, peel off another skin, and wash them in cold water. Next boil them in milk until tender all through, so that you can easily pierce them with a needle; drain off the milk; measure them, and to a quart of onions, allow a quart of the best cider vinegar. Boil in the vinegar two muslin bags with broken up nutmeg and mace. When it has boiled, pour it hot over the onions in the jar. Lay one bag at the bottom, and one in the middle. Finish with one tablespoonful of salad oil, cork the jar immediately, and tie on a leather cover.

CUCUMBER PICKLES.—Without vinegar. Take nice, green, good sized cucumbers; when you wash them, notice how many quarts of water it takes to cover them well. Then take a stone jar or keg, cover the bottom with grape leaves, then put a layer of cucumbers, some whole black peppers, quite a handful of fresh fennel, a few laurel leaves, if you have them, then a layer of cucumbers, and so on, until the jar is filled; cover the top with grape leaves, and put little sticks across to keep them down. Then take as many quarts of water, and two over, as it took to wash them. Put to each quart a handful of salt; then boil the water, set it off to cool, and when it is cool, pour it over the pickles; after standing in the cellar about two weeks they will be nearly as sour as vinegar pickles, and are excellent. The white scum that forms over them must always be removed.

MRS. S. H——.

VINEGAR PICKLES.—Take small cucumbers, wash them and put them in a brine strong enough to float an egg; also take small, white onions, as many as you like—so that you can use alternate layers of cucumbers and onions. Let them both stand in the brine three days; then take them out and wipe them dry. Have your glass jars ready, and put in the bottom one grape leaf, then a layer of cucumbers, and then the onions; season with white mustard seed, black and red peppers, a little fennel, fresh from the garden, a few laurel leaves and a very few cloves. Season every layer in this way, until the jar is full, then put in a few pieces of horse-radish and one grape leaf. Fill the jars with the best boiling cider vinegar.

MRS. S. H——.

TO USE UP RANCID BUTTER.—Take the butter and put it into a vessel on the stove; fill it only half full, and *watch closely,* as it will rise up when it gets near boiling; if necessary lift it off quickly, lest it should boil over and get on fire. Unless the butter is *very* old it will not rise much. Stir it very often. The grounds that settle at the bottom will get a light brown, *when* the butter is done. After standing a few minutes, it can be emptied into a jar; be very careful not to get the settlings in. It will keep a year or more and is *very* nice for baking, cooking, &c., &c.

MRS. S. H——.

CORN STARCH BLANC MANGE.—Boil one pint of milk; sweeten to taste. Dissolve two tablespoonfuls of corn starch in some cold milk, and stir in the boiling milk; stir *constantly* until thick. Flavor with vanilla, and pour into a dish or mould. To be eaten cold with whipped cream.

MRS. EVA S——.

SPONGE CAKE.—Six eggs beaten separately, a saucer of sugar and a saucer of flour; beat the yolks and sugar well, add flour, and, last, the whites; stir just long enough to mix well, and no longer; flavor with lemon or vanilla.

MRS. EVA S——.

TAPIOCA PUDDING.—Soak eight tablespoons of tapioca in one quart of warm milk till it is soft; then add two tablespoons of melted butter, five eggs well beaten, with spice and sugar to taste. Bake in a buttered dish.

MRS. EVA S——.

BOILED FROSTING.—The whites of three eggs, beaten to a stiff froth, one large cup of granulated sugar moistened with four tablespoons of hot water; boil the sugar briskly for five minutes, or until it ropes when dropped from the spoon; then, with the left hand, pour the boiling syrup upon the beaten eggs, in a small stream, while beating with the right hand. If preferred, add one cup of hickory nut kernels chopped fine.

CANNED CURRANTS.—Look them over carefully, stem and weigh them, allowing a pound of sugar to a pound of fruit; put them into a kettle, cover and leave them to heat slowly. Stew gently for twenty or thirty minutes, then add sugar, and shake the kettle occasionally to make it mix with the fruit. Do not boil it, but keep it as hot as possible, until all the sugar is dissolved; pour it into cans, and cover it at once.

BOTTLED CIDER.—Take good, sweet cider, heat it to the boiling point, *but do not boil it.* Pour it into jugs or bottles, with two or three raisins in each, and seal them while hot. It will keep all winter.

SHERBERT.—One pine-apple, four lemons, two quarts of water, two teacups of sugar. Steep the pine-apple in the water for two hours, then strain, add the juice of the lemons and the sugar. Whip the white of five eggs, with three tablespoons of sugar; turn *all* into the freezer, and freeze at once. *Excellent.*

FOR THE TOILET.

SCRAPE one cake of brown Windsor soap to a powder; add one ounce of lemon juice, and one ounce of cologne. Mix well and form into cakes. Excellent for sunburn.

COLD CREAM.—Half an ounce of spermaceti, twenty grains of white wax, two ounces of pure oil of sweet almonds, half an ounce of pure glycerine, and six drops of oil of rose. Melt the first *three* ingredients together, and, when cooling, add the glycerine and oil of rose, stirring until cold.

BEST TOOTH POWDER.—Rub the teeth well with prepared chalk, and then brush them with pure white castile soap and tepid water.

FOR ROUGH SKIN, HIVES, &c.—One ounce of glycerine, half an ounce of rosemary water, twenty drops of carbolic acid and a few drops of ottar of roses.

TO WHITEN THE HANDS.—One wineglass of cologne, and one wineglass of lemon juice, strained clear; scrape two cakes Windsor soap to a powder, and mix all together in a mould. When hard it is fit for use, and will be found excellent for whitening the hands.

A Splendid Bath Powder.—Two and a half drachms of camphor, four ounces orris root, and sixteen ounces starch, reduced to impalpable powder; tie in a coarse muslin bag.

For Heat.—A teaspoon of carbolic acid in a pint of rose water.

A Fine Cologne.—One gallon of deodorized alcohol, one ounce of oil of lavender, one ounce of oil of orange, two drachms of oil of cedrat, one drachm of oil of orange flowers, one drachm of oil of rose, and one drachm of oil of ambergris; mix well and keep in a cool place three weeks.

Splendid Toilet Water.—One drachm each of oil of bergamot, lavender and lemon, ten drops each of oil of jasmine and rose and essence of ambergris, and one pint of spirits of wine. Mix and keep well closed, in a cool place, for two months, when it will be ready for use.

Glycerine For the Toilet.—Two ounces distilled water, one ounce glycerine, one ounce alcohol, half an ounce tincture of benzoin, and one grain of carmine.

USEFUL KNOWLEDGE.

BUCKWHEAT BATTER spread over grease spots on a carpet, and let remain until dry, and then wiped off, will take out the grease nicely. Repeat the process if necessary.

MERCURIAL OINTMENT, made soft with coal oil, is certain death to bed-bugs. Oil of cedar is, perhaps, a pleasanter remedy.

APPLES keep well in winter, if placed in barrels or boxes, with a layer of autumn leaves alternating with a layer of apples, until the box is full. They should be put in the cellar *only* in time to escape freezing.

A PAN OF HOT WATER set in the oven will prevent cakes and bread from scorching.

ORANGE AND LEMON PEEL.—Dry and pound it, and keep in corked bottles.

TEA should be ground like coffee, or crushed, before pouring boiling water on it.

ARTICLES MADE OF ZEPHYR, are cleaned by rubbing in flour, or magnesia, changing often. Shake off the flour and hang the article in the open air a short time.

Wash Boilers are best cleaned, by washing them with sweet milk, or greasing them with lard.

Fine Starch is made by wetting two or three tablespoons of starch smooth with a little cold water, then pouring on a quart of boiling water, stirring rapidly all the time: place it on the stove, and let it boil about five minutes, stirring frequently; add a little salt, a piece of butter, a piece of a sperm candle, or a little coal oil.

Cold Starch is best made with soap suds instead of clear water, using toilet soap. Use one teaspoon (not heaping nor level) of starch to one pint of water.

Irons that are rusty can be improved by rubbing well, the night before using, with coal oil. If necessary, rub them over salt and *powdered* bath brick mixed.

Best Washerwomen do not use cold starch for shirts and collars; they hang them on the line before being starched, and, after they are dry, starch them in *very thin* hot starch, roll them up and lay them aside, until ready to be ironed.

Whitewash for Cellars.—One ounce of carbolic acid to one gallon of whitewash, or add copperas to whitewash until it is yellow. Copperas is a fine disinfectant, and drives away vermin.

Parsley can be kept fresh by putting it into a strong boiling brine, and then hanging it up and drying it in bunches, in a dry cellar or store room, with blossom downward.

CABBAGE FOR WINTER USE should be buried in rows two and two, not quite touching; each two one or two feet apart, root downward. In this way, none are exposed except those to be taken up.

In broiling meat, when the coals blaze up too much, sprinkle salt on them.

ZINC can be best cleaned by rubbing fresh lard on it with a cloth, and then rubbing it dry.

GREASE can be removed from garments by dissolving one tablespoon of salt in four tablespoons of alcohol,—shaking the mixture well and applying it with a sponge.

CASHMERE is best cleaned by washing it in hot suds, with borax in the water, rinsing in bluing water, made *very blue*, and ironing while damp.

RIBBONS should be washed in cold soap-suds, and not rinsed.

BUTTER can be kept nicely, without ice, by inverting a large crock (not glazed) over the dish of butter, and wrapping the crock with a wet cloth, with a little water in the dish of butter.

VALUE OF FOREIGN MONEY IN U. S. CURRENCY.

One pound sterling of England,				$ 4.84
" guinea,				5.05
" crown	"	"		1.21
" shilling	"	"		.22

One napoleon of France,	3.84
Five francs, "	.93
One franc, "	.18½
" florin, "	48½
" thaler of Saxony,	.08
" guilder of Netherlands,	.40
" ducat of Austria,	2.28
" doubloon of Spain,	15.54
" real,	.05
Five rubles of Russia,	3.95
One ruble,	.75
" franc of Belgium,	.18½
" ducat of Bavaria,	2.27
" franc of Switzerland,	18½
" crown of Tuscany.	1.05½

WEIGHTS TO THE BUSHEL.

58 pounds of	shelled corn	make 1 bushel.	
56 "	rye,	"	"
46 "	barley,	"	"
60 "	wheat,	"	"
70 "	corn on the cob,	"	"
52 "	buckwheat,	"	"
32 "	oats,	"	"
20 "	bran,	"	"
45 "	clover seed,	"	"
60 "	timothy, "	"	"
56 "	flax, "	"	"
45 "	hemp, "	"	"

14 pounds of blue-grass seed, make 1 bushel.
60 " Irish potatoes, " "
50 " sweet potatoes, " "
57 " onions, " "
62 " beans, " "
24 " dried apples, " "
33 " dried peaches peeled, " "
36 " " unpeeled, " "

OUR PRESIDENTS.

	Born.	Died.	Ruled.
Geo. Washington, Va.,	Feb. 22, 1732.	Dec. 14, 1899.	8 years.
Jno. Adams, Mass.	Oct. 29, 1751.	July 4, 1826.	4 "
Thos. Jefferson, Va.,	Apr. 2, 1743.	July 4, 1826.	8 "
Jas. Madison, Va.,	March 16, 1751.	June 28, 1836.	8 "
Jas. Monroe, Va.,	April 28, 1758.	July 4, 1831.	8 "
Jno. Q. Adams, Mass.,	July 11, 1767.	Feb, 23, 1848.	4 "
Andrew Jackson, Tenn.,	March, 15, 1767.	June 8, 1845.	8 "
Martin Van Buren, N. Y.	Dec. 5, 1782.	July 24, 1862.	4 "
Wm. H. Harrison, O.,	Feb. 9, 1773.	April 4, 1841.	1 month.
Jno. Tyler, Va.,	March 29, 1790.	Jan'y 17, 1862.	3 yrs, 11 mos.
Jas. K. Polk, Tenn.,	Nov. 2, 1795.	June 15, 1849.	4 "
Zachary Taylor, La.,	Nov. 24, 1784.	July 9, 1851.	1 " 4 mos.
Millard Fillmore, N Y.,	Jan. 7, 1800.	March 8, 1874.	2 " 8 "
Franklin Pierce. N. H.,	Nov. 23, 1804.	Oct. 8, 1869.	4 "
Jas. Buchanan, Pa.,	Apr. 22, 1791.	June 1, 1868.	4 "
Abraham Lincoln, Ill.,	Feb. 15, 1809.	April 15, 1865.	4 " 1 mo., 11ds.
Andrew Johnson, Tenn.,	Dec. 29, 1808.	July 31, 1875.	3 " 10 mos.,19ds.
U. S. Grant, Illinois,	April 27, 1822.	———.	8 "
R. B. Hayes, Ohio,	Oct. 4, 1822.	———.	4 "
James A. Garfield, Ohio,	Nov. 19, 1831.	———.	———.

INDEX

Almond Cake, Mrs. M. E. Caldwell,........................ 85
Angel Cake, Mrs. C. V. Jaquith,......................... 95
Ants, To get rid of,.....................................132
Apples, a-la-Turque,.....................................104
Apple Batter Pudding....................................104
Apple Butter, Mrs. Geo. Levings,........................ 64
Apple Charlotte, Snow,..................................111
Apple Custard Pie,......................................118
Apple Dumplings, Baked, Boiled,.........................110
Apple Fritters,...141
Apple, (green) Pie, Meringue,...........................118
Apples, to keep,..149
Apple Sauce,.. 63
Asparagus Omelette 29
Aunt Angie's Black or Fruit Cake, Mrs. William Harding, 92
Bachelor's Buttons,.....................................100
Bake Day Pudding,.......................................109
Baked Beans,..125
Baked Ham,..143
Baking Powder Biscuits, Mesdames Matthias and Brown, 79
Baked Trout or Blue Fish, ... 12
Barley, Pearl...139
Barley Water...139
Bath Powder, ... 149
Bath Tub, to brighten,..................................132
Batter Pudding, Steamed,................................109
Beans and Oysters,...................................... 20
Bed Bugs, to destroy,...............................133, 149
Beef Broth, with tapioca,...............................137
Beef, Dry, and to Corn, and to Preserve, ...38, 40

Beef, Roast	36
Beefsteak, a-la-Mock-Duck,	38
Beefsteak, Fried, Broiled, Mrs. Hamburger,	36, 37
Beefsteak, Fried,	143
Beefsteak, Hamburg, Mrs. Hamburger	36
Beets, Plain, Sweet Pickle,	125, 144
Berry Short Cake,	97
Birds, Bread Sauce, for,	49, 55
Bits of Hominy, Meat etc.,	23
Blackberry Cordial,	71, 72
Black Cake, Mrs. M. P. Jaquith,	92
Black Cashmere, to clean,	152
Bombay Pudding,	105
Boston Pound Cake, Mrs. S. Hamburger,	90
Bottled Cider,	148
Brandy Peaches, Mrs. Hamburger,	67
Bread, Mrs. Tanner,	74, 75, 140
Bread and Butter Pudding	105
Bread Omelette,	28
Breakfast and Supper,	21
Breakfast Cakes, Rolls,	23, 81, 141
Breakfast Dish, and Stew,	22, 23
Brown Bread, Steamed,	77
Brushes,	6
Buckwheat Cakes,	80, 141
Bunions, to cure,	136
Bunn Pudding,	105
Bunns,	78
Burns, Remedy for	135
Cabbage, stuffed, Miss Kate Rudy,	122
Cakes—To keep fresh,	82, 134
Candy—Horehound, Molasses, Sugar, Black Crook, Cocoanut, Cream, Lemon, Butter Scotch, Splendid,	127, 128
Canned Cherries	69
Canned Corn, Mrs. Sheppard, Mrs. Levings,	124
Canning Large Fruits,	68, 133
Caramel Cake,	88
Cauliflower,	125
Celery Flavoring,	56

INDEX.

Celery, Stewed, Sauce,	54, 126
Celery Slaw,	122
Cement,	130
Chamois Skin, to wash,	131
Champagne Cider—Sweet,	73
Charlotte Russe, Mrs. W. S. Harding,	111
Cheap Wine for Cooking,	73
Cheese Omelette,	29
Cheese Relish,	30
Cherry Bounce,	72
Chicken, a-la-mode, Mrs. C. W. Levings,	48
Chicken Jelly,	137
Chicken Young—Fricassee, Steamed,	48, 142
Chicken Salad,	52, 53
Chilblains, how to relieve,	136
Chili Sauce,	51, 60, 61
Chills and Fever,	133
Chocolate,	32, 128
Chocolate Custard, Caramels,	106, 128
Cholera Cure,	135
Chow Chow,	61, 63
Christmas Pudding,	106
Citron Melon Preserves,	67
Cocoa,	32
Cocoanut Rose Cake, Mrs. M. E. Caldwell,	85, 95
Cocoanut Pie, Mrs. G. S. Brecount, Drops,	119, 127
Coffee,	32
Coffee Cake,	82, 84
Cold Sauce,	50
Cold Slaw,	122
Cologne,	149
Cookies, Mesdames Matthias, Levings, Harding,	97, 98, 163
Corn Bread,	79, 81
Corn Fritters,	25
Corn Oysters, Mrs. J. C. Jones,	123
Corn Starch Blanc Mange,	146
Corn Starch Cake, Merangue Pudding,	93, 108
Cottage Pudding,	104
Crab Apple, Siberian, preserves,	67

Creamed Biscuits,	76
Cream Cake, Mrs. Connelly's,	88
Cream Cake, No. 2, Mrs. W. H.,	89
Creamed Crackers,	138
Cream Oysters on Half Shell,	16
Cream or Milk Toast,	21
Cream Pie, Nos. 1 and 2,	115
Cream Puffs, Mrs. Hamburger,	80
Cream Sponge Cake, Mrs. C. W. Levings,	83
Croquets, Mrs. Kate Rudy,	27
Crumb Cakes,	80
Cucumber Catsup, Mrs. J. H. Matthias,	60
Cucumber Pickles,	58, 144
Cucumber Salad, Fried,	25
Curing Hams, Curing Feet, Pork, Mutton & Tongue,	45, 143
Currants, Canned,	148
Currant Cake, Mrs. S. S. Levings,	93
Currant or Cherry Sauce, Mrs. C. W. Levings,	57
Currant Wine,	72
Custard, Cake, Pudding, Pie,	90, 106, 117
Custard, Chocolate,	106
Cut Flowers, to keep,	135
Danish Pudding, Mrs. Kate Rudy,	103
Delicate Cake, Mrs. M. P. Jacquith,	91
Delmonico Sauce,	27
Diphtheria, Remedy for,	136
Dolly Varden Cake, Mrs. W. S. Harding,	89
Double-quick Pudding, Mrs. J. C. Jones,	103
Doughnuts, French, Mrs. C. V. Jaquith, Mrs. Brecount,	99
Drawers, to keep from swelling,	133
Drawn Butter Sauce,	55
Dressing for Fowls, Mrs. S. Hamburger,	47
Dried Yeast, Mrs. Joe Payne,	74
Drinks	32
Drop Cakes,	100
Dry Bread, Biscuits, Cakes,	23
Dumplings, for soup, Mrs. S. Hamburger	10
Eggs. Omelette, Baked, Fried, for lunch, Scrambled, Scalloped, To boil,	27, 30, 134

English mixed pickles, ... 61
Eve's Pudding, ... 107
Fancy Desserts, ... 111
Farmer's Pudding, ... 109
Feather Cake, Mrs. M. P. Jacquith, ... 92
Fig Cake, Mrs. J. H. Matthias, Mrs. M. P. Jaquith, ... 86
Fig Pudding, Mrs. M. P. Jacquith, ... 103
Fillet-de-boeuf, Mrs. Hamburger, ... 36
Fish, Boiled, Fried, Broiled, Mrs. F. M. Patterson, ... 12, 13
Flannel Cakes, Rolls, ... 78, 81
Flies, to destroy 132
Foam Sauce, ... 52
Foreign Coin, ... 152
Fowls, ... 46
French Croquettes, ... 28
Fresh Peaches, ... 66
Fricadelles, Mrs. Hamburger, ... 26
Fricassee Chicken, Calf's Tongue, Young Chicken, ... 44, 48
Frozen Pudding, Plants, Feet, ... 107, 134, 136
Fruit Cake, Blanc Mange, Mrs. Hamburger, ... 84, 91, 138
Fruit, To Spice, ... 64, 67
Furniture Polish, ... 130
Ginger Cakes, Snaps, Mrs. S. S. Levings, Mrs. Matthias, 98, 99
Glycerine for the Toilet, ... 149
Gooseberry Catsup, ... 57
Goose, To Roast a, Mrs. Hamburger, ... 47
Gold Cake, Mrs. M. P. Jacquith, ... 88
Graham Bread, Gems, Mush, ... 22, 77, 80, 81
Grape Butter, Spiced, ... 68
Grape Wine, ... 72
Grated Ham Sandwiches, ... 29
Grease Spots, To Remove, ... 133
Green Corn Pudding, ... 123
Green Tomatoes, Fried, ... 25
Hair, Care of, ... 135
Ham, Baked, Stuffed, Sandwiches, Omelette, ... 29, 30, 44
Ham, Boiled, Mrs. Brecount. 45
Hands to whiten, ... 148
Hash, Mrs. Brown, ... 24

Hay Fever, To cure,	134
Hen's Nest,	113
Hickory Nut Cake, Mrs. Brecount,	94
Hives,	148
Hop Yeast, Dry, Mrs. Dr. Smith,	74
Ice Cream, Mrs. Geo. Hunt,	111, 112
Ice Cream Cake, Mrs. Caldwell,	84
Iceland Moss Blanc Mange,	138
Iced Tea,	33
Icing, Boiled,	86, 96, 147
Irish Potato Pudding,	108
Iron Ware,	6
Jam—Blackberry, Raspberry or Strawberry,	70
Jellies — Apple, Cider, Crab Apple, Currant, Grape, Quince, Wine,	69, 70, 71
Jumbles, Mrs. Jacquith and others,	99, 100
Kentucky Biscuits,	81
Lady Fingers,	100
Lamb's Liver,	41
Lard, How to keep,	133
Lemon Butter, Lemon Drops, Lemon Extract,	57, 68, 129
Lemon Gelatine, Mrs. Wm. Harding,	71
Lemon Sauce, Paste,	50, 96
Lemon Pie, Mesdames Payne, Jacquith, Matthias, Sheppard and Levings,	116, 117
Lemon Pudding, Meringue, Mrs. Hamburger,	102, 107
Loaf Cake, Mrs. M. P. Jacquith,	92
Luncheon Cake,	78
Lunch for Traveling,	45
Maccaroons,	101
Maccaroni, Baked, Boiled,	124, 125
Mangoes,	60
Marble, To clean,	132
Mayonnaise Sauce,	54, 56
Meats,	35
Meat Scallops,	27
Meerschaum Pipe, To cleanse,	131
Mince Meat,	114
Minced Meat on Toast,	27

INDEX.

Miscellaneous Knowledge, ... 130
Mirrors, Where not to hang, ... 132
Mock Duck, ... 143
Moth Patches, To remove, ... 134
Mush, ... 22
Mushrooms, Stewed, ... 124
Muskmelons, Preserved, ... 65
Mustard, To mix, Mrs. C. W. Levings, ... 55
Noodles, How to make, ... 7
Oatmeal, Soup, ... 22, 8
Orange Cake, Mrs. Brecount, Pudding, ... 94, 107
Orange Gelatine, Pudding, Cream, ... 71, 107, 112
Ostrich Plumes, To cleanse 131
Oysters and Beans, ... 20
Oysters, Broiled, Panned, Stewed, ... 16, 17
Oyster Omelette, Salad, Macaroni, ... 19, 125
Oysters on shell, Scalloped, Fried, On toast, ... 15, 17, 18, 19
Oyster Soup, Mrs. Magner, ... 9, 15
Pansies, ... 131
Pastry for pies, Mrs. Wm. Harding, ... 114
Parker House Rolls, ... 76
Parsnep Fritters, ... 26
Pawn House, ... 22
Peaches, Spiced, Preserved, Brandy, ... 65, 67, 68
Pearls, To keep brilliant 135
Pearl Barley, ... 139
Pears, Preserved, ... 66
Peppermint Drops, ... 127, 129
Pickles, ... 50
Pickled Tongue, Mrs. Hamburger, ... 40
Pickled Onions, ... 144
Pie Crust, ... 142
Pies, ... 114
Pine Apple pie 118
Plain Toast, Mrs. Brown, ... 21
Plum Cake, ... 93
Pone-De-Tat, Mrs. K. Rudy, ... 121
Pop Corn Balls 129
Pop Overs, ... 81

Potato Balls, ... 29
Potato Edging for Tongues, ... 41
Potato Pancakes, Mrs. Hamburger, ... 26
Potatoes, Baked, Whipped, Mashed, Scallopped, ... 120, 121
Potato Puddings, ... 108
Potato Salad, ... 56
Prairie Chickens, ... 143
Puddings, ... 102
Pudding, A nice, ... 109
Pudding Sauce, ... 51
Puff Paste, ... 114
Puff Pudding, ... 110
Pumpkin Pie, Mrs. S. S. Levings, ... 117
Presidents, Table of, ... 154
Quails, ... 143
Quinces, Preserved whole, ... 66
Quince Cordial, ... 72
Raisins, About washing, ... 134
Raisin Pie, ... 118
Rancid Butter, To use, ... 145
Refrigerator, To purify, ... 131
Renovating Mixture, ... 133
Ribbon Cake, ... 90
Roast Turkey, Goose, Mrs. Hamburger, ... 46, 47
Rough Skin, ... 148
Rusk, ... 78
Salad Dressing, Mrs. M. Jacquith, ... 51, 52
Salt Rising Yeast, ... 74, 75
Sand Tarts, ... 100
Sauce for Puddings, ... 50, 52
Sauce for Salads, Mrs. Rudy, ... 50
Sauces—Rhubarb, Celery, Horse Radish, ... 50, 51
Sausage, ... 44
Scotch Cookies, and Cakes ... 98, 99
Scotch Stew, ... 24
Seal Brown Cake, ... 83
Sherbert, ... 147
Sick Room, ... 137

INDEX.

Silver Cake, Mrs. M. P. Jacquith,	88
Silver Polish,	131
Sleeplessness, To relieve,	136
Small Cakes and Cookies,	97
Small Pox Cure,	136
Smoked Halibut,	13
Snow Cake,	84, 88
Snow Pudding, Mrs. Jacquith,	103
Soap,	133
Soda Biscuits,	77
Soda Cream,	34
Soups—Barley, Chicken, Corn, Farina, French, Green Pea, Noodle, Oatmeal, Tomato and Oyster, Mrs. Hamburger,	7, 8, 11
Soups—Tomato, Oyster, Mrs. Magner,	9
Sponge Cake,	82, 83
Sponge for Winter use,	140
Sponge Roll,	82
Stains, To remove,	132
Steamed Chicken,	142
Stone Ware,	6
Stove, To keep from rusting,	132
Succotash,	123
Sugar Drops,	100
Sugar, To brown for sauce,	134
Suet Pudding, Mrs. Jacquith, Mrs. Rudy,	103
Sweetbreads, Fried, Stewed, Boiled,	42, 43
Sweet Pickles,	64, 65
Sweet Potatoes,	121
Sweet Potato Pudding,	108
Taffy,	129
Tapioca, Cream, Jelly, Pudding,	112, 136, 146
Tea,	33, 150
Tin Ware,	5
Toilet Water,	149
Tomatoes, Stewed, Scalloped, Stuffed, Baked,	122, 123
Tomato Catsup, Mrs. Levings and others,	57, 59, 62
Tomato Omelette,	29
Tomato Pickles,	58, 59, 60, 61, 62, 65

Tongue, Stewed,	41
Tomato Soy,	62
Tripe-a-la-creole, Stewed,	42
Tomato Pies,	119
Utensils for the kitchen	5
Vanilla Extract,	56
Veal steak, cutlets, salad,	38. 55
Veal Omelette, Mrs. Brecount,	39
Veal Patties. Mrs. C. W. Levings,	39
Vegetables,	120
Venison, Steak, Roast, Gravy, Pie,	43, 44
Velvet Cake,	93
Vienna Rolls, Mrs. Magner,	76
Vinegar Pickles,	145
Washing Fluid, and how to wash,	130, 132
Weights and Measures, Table of,	4
Whipped Cream, Miss Anna Caldwell,	112
White Cake, Mrs. Harding and others,	87
White Mountain Cake,	84, 86
Whites of eggs, to beat quickly,	134
Wine Jelly, Mrs. Wm. Harding,	71
Wine Sauce,	54
Wooden Ware	5
Zamtiftige Tarte, Mrs. Hamburger,	91

www.ingramcontent.com/pod-product-compliance
Lightning Source LLC
Chambersburg PA
CBHW030253170426
43202CB00009B/720